798.23 British Horse
Society.

The instructor's
handbook

$ 4.50

THE
INSTRUCTORS' HANDBOOK

by

THE BRITISH HORSE SOCIETY

and

THE PONY CLUB

The British Horse Society
National Equestrian Centre
Kenilworth, Warwickshire, CV8 2LR

Published in 1977 by
BARRON'S
Woodbury, New York

CJMS -1

First Edition   1955
Second Edition 1961
Third Edition   1964
Fourth Edition 1968

Published in 1977 by
Barron's Educational Series, Inc.
113 Crossways Park Drive
Woodbury, New York 11797

Library of Congress Catalog Card No. 76-55317

Library of Congress Cataloging in Publication Data
British Horse Society.
    The instructor's handbook.
    Includes index.
    1. Horsemanship—Study and teaching. I. Pony Club. II. Title.
SF310.5.B74 1976 798'.23 76-55317
ISBN 0-8120-5125-4
ISBN 0-8120-0753-0 pbk.

Cloth Edition
International Standard Book N. 0-8120-5125-4

PRINTED IN THE UNITED STATES OF AMERICA

CONTENTS

CONTENTS

LIST OF ILLUSTRATIONS

v

FOREWORD

This handbook, adopted for instructors of the British Horse Society and the Pony Club, was originally produced for the Pony Club when it became clear that the traditional source of instructors was drying up and that in the future the Pony Club would have to train its own instructors. It was therefore written in simple form largely for the use of those who had little experience of instructing and who found themselves responsible for teaching groups of young people.

In the ensuing twelve years great progress has been made in the training of instructors both in the Pony Club and in the Riding Clubs. Ideas and methods have changed and developed. Moreover the Riding Clubs and even the Pony Club are not dealing solely with children; the standard at the top has risen to international form.

In this, the fourth edition, more advanced teaching is included following the elementary instruction.

A Branch or Club with sufficient, qualified instructors will have little difficulty in attracting and teaching members, provided an effective syllabus is followed. The only way in which to train the required number of instructors is by holding central and local courses and conferences.

It is hoped that this edition will assist in continuing and developing a sound system of teaching which is so essential if riding is to improve and prosper. In instances where the pronouns *he* and *him* appear, they have been used to avoid awkward prose. It should be understood that these references apply to *all* instructors and riders, whether male or female.

I. SUGGESTIONS FOR INSTRUCTORS

1. LEARNING

Young people will only come to Pony Club Rallies if they enjoy themselves and if they think they can learn something from them. Whether or not they come, therefore, depends upon our instructors.

Nobody can be forced to learn; there must be a desire to do so. Young people will only learn if they are interested, if there is an incentive and if they can see the reason for what they are doing.

2. TEACHING

The first necessity in an instructor is an understanding of young people and the ability to arouse their interest and enthusiasm.

He must know more of the subject than he is expected to teach. Pupils will soon realise whether or not he has a real knowledge of his subject, even if no awkward questions are asked.

A minimum knowledge of the subject, as far as the Pony Club is concerned, entails knowing the contents of the Pony Club books. The "Manual of Horsemanship" and "Training the Young Pony" contain *what is taught*; "The Instructors' Handbook" indicates *how to teach it*.

1

3. PRINCIPLES OF GOOD INSTRUCTION

Instruction is an art and not an exact science. A thorough knowledge of the subject is the first essential for an instructor, who should ride well enough to give simple demonstrations and to manage an awkward pony.

Instructors will have to study and work at the art of instruction; to learn this entails attendance at a course—local or otherwise—and plenty of practice.

The following principles should be taken as a guide and applied with common sense according to circumstances:

(i) Always know what you are *Aiming at* and the *Object* of your lesson.

(ii) Be *as Simple, Clear* and *Definite* as you can.

(iii) Prepare your lesson beforehand. Study the syllabus, read the textbook and know exactly what you intend to teach.
The success of a lesson depends largely upon the trouble taken in preparation beforehand.

(iv) Use the right senses. *Hearing, sight* and *feel*—the latter is very important in riding. The more senses involved the greater will be the impression on the pupil, e.g., hearing and sight are better than hearing alone.

A good lesson should be:

Hearing (Explanation)   5 mins.
Sight   (Demonstration)   10 mins.
Feel   (Practice)   45 mins.
AVOID TOO MUCH TALK.

(v) Keep up the interest of the Ride; keep them active.

(vi) You must understand young people and be human.
Be firm but sympathetic—especially with nervous pupils.
Be patient and quiet.   Be natural.

Encourage by praise, when deserved, especially with small children and beginners.

Have no favourites. Keep order.

NEVER be sarcastic; DO NOT bully.

You and your horse must be well turned out and an example to the Ride.

(vii) CONFIRM by practical tests and by questions that your Ride has mastered one stage before going on to the next.

(viii) Insist on punctuality and always be punctual yourself. The late arrival of an instructor can disorganise the entire arrangements for instruction.

4. VARIOUS WAYS OF INSTRUCTING

(i) **The Lesson.** This is the most effective way of instructing. The essence of the lesson is PRACTICE. Demonstrations and explanations must be short—just sufficient to teach the movements. When possible, correct mistakes by question and answer.

Members of the ride may be asked to comment: this will help to maintain interest and to show how to learn from the achievements and mistakes of others.

(ii) **The Demonstration.** This should be part of every lesson; it is essential in teaching riding and horsemanship and should follow a simple explanation, thus appealing to two senses at once. If dismounted, the Instructor should have an assistant to give the demonstration while he explains. "The eye is the window to the brain."

(iii) **The Lecture.** Lectures enable the Instructor to teach facts when time is short and numbers are large. The Instructor should be clear about what he wants to teach and should not include too much subject matter. He should make use of film-strips, diagrams, models and any other visual aids which will add interest. Lectures should be kept short—30 to 40 minutes —and should be followed by questions and a discussion to ensure that the main lessons have been absorbed.

(iv) **Discussion, Question and Answer.** Where the majority of the class have some knowledge of the subject, this is an effective way of teaching. It keeps the members of the class "on their toes" and they enjoy being able to give the correct answer. This method can be used at the end of a lecture or during a rest period of a ride or at any time when a class needs "waking up."

(v) **The Film.** Motion films, especially if they include a commentary, are most useful for teaching riding, as in addition to showing the correct positions and movements, they can demonstrate timing and rhythm which are so important. If good, they create tremendous interest, especially when they show well-known experts in action. They are also useful as a means of studying the action and movements of a horse and of teaching Horsemastership.

(vi) **The Book.** Members of a class are given a copy of the book and are called upon in turn to read aloud the selected section. The Instructor makes frequent interruptions to elaborate points or to give demonstrations of what is meant.

This method is useful for the intensive training of candidates for Tests and is very convenient for teaching horsemastership and similar subjects.

The importance of reading as a means of learning should be stressed. Instructors and members must know "The Manual of Horsemanship".

(vii) **The Quiz.** This can be run individually or between teams so making use of the competitive spirit. The instructor can prepare and ask questions or, better, the teams can be given a portion of the "Manual" from which to prepare and ask their own questions.

Remembering that "what we have to do we can only learn by doing", an instructor has to decide upon the best way of teaching a particular lesson. Practice is most important but this must be supplemented and varied according to what has to be taught and to circumstances—weather, the time of the year, the need for rest and change, and the availability of films, models, &c.

But the Instructor must always think out the best way of teaching a particular lesson at a particular moment.

5. GIVING A RIDING LESSON

(i) When giving a riding lesson, except with the very young or when giving specialised instruction, it is desirable that either the Instructor or an assistant be mounted on a horse sufficiently well trained to be able to give the required demonstrations. He should always adopt a correct position whether standing still or on the move.

(ii) At all times the Instructor should place himself where he can best see and be seen and heard. The Ride or class should be made as comfortable as possible when standing still and situated where they can see and hear, e.g. downwind and backs to the sun, when outside. Horsemastership classes should only consist of as many as can see.

In a school the Instructor, if mounted, should be a few yards from one end and just off the centre line. The same applies in a manege except that he may often stand outside in this case. He should vary his position according to the work to be done and to the conditions.

A convenient position for the Ride during talks and demonstrations is in a semicircle at the end of the manege (see Figure 4), otherwise they may stand in line (see Figures 5a and 5b).

(iii) It is best to take a Ride in a rectangular manege.

(iv) All practical lessons should follow this sequence:

(a) *Preparation*

The Instructor prepares the lesson he is to teach. He ensures that he has the appliances, e.g., manege, jumps, grooming kit, etc., necessary for the lesson.

The Ride is placed in the most advantageous position.

(b) *Explanation*

The Instructor gives a short explanation of the exercise or lesson and its objects. This should be very brief and clear.

(c) *Demonstration*

The Instructor demonstrates the correct way, explaining what he is doing at the same time.

(d) *Application or Practice*

The Ride carries out the exercise.

(e) *Demonstration*

The Instructor demonstrates the chief faults followed immediately by the correct method, which must be the impression taken away by the pupil.

(f) *Repetition*

The Ride carries out the exercise once more and the Instructor corrects faults in individuals as they occur.

(g) *Confirmation*

Confirm by tests and questions that the Ride has mastered the lesson.

Some typical lessons are given in Appendices I to V. These lessons are based on the general principles described above and have stood the test of time. It is easy for an Instructor to work out a lesson on these lines on any subject which has to be taught.

The intention in making the above suggestions and producing typical lessons is to help instructors, particularly those who are young or inexperienced. With practice, instructors will develop their own ways of teaching and of creating and maintaining interest. There is no intention here to be dogmatic, provided teaching is on sound lines and in accordance with the Pony Club doctrine. Much use can be made of games, displays and competitions to stimulate enthusiasm and to improve performance. Above all, members should *enjoy* the instruction and the rallies.

6. GENERAL CONSIDERATIONS

(i) In general the would-be rider notes the performance of a person whose prowess he admires; this creates sufficient interest to encourage him to try himself. He may attempt to learn by a system of trial and error, but this may lead to much wasteful effort and discouragement.

Here occurs the opportunity for the trained instructor who will follow, with more or less variation, the principles and methods already referred to in this book. Above all the interest must be maintained and the pupil must enjoy riding. When dealing with young children, games, particularly those in which lessons are unconsciously learnt, should occupy most of the time; instruction must never be dull.

(ii) Teaching must follow a sequence; ideally each lesson should be related to those that have gone before and those that are to follow. This is difficult to attain in Pony Club Branches except in camp or on courses where continuity can be assured. Here a scheme of work must be planned, covering the whole series of rides, with detailed preparation for each day. This involves careful thought of what to teach and the best way to set about it. The syllabus at the end of this book will give some help. It will be necessary to break down a complex movement into its simpler component parts, finding words to describe what is being done so that the explanation is precise and simple.

Learning does not follow a smooth uninterrupted course— sometimes it speeds along, sometimes it is retarded. No two people learn at the same rate due to many factors, so that considerable individual attention is essential. It becomes more difficult to maintain a lively interest in a large number of pupils so that a Ride ideally should consist of not more than eight people.

(iii) Riding is a skill and has several characteristics among which are accuracy, balance, rhythm, smoothness, fluency and co-ordination. A high level of performance must be attained in elementary activities such as leading in hand, mounting, keeping correct distances in Rides and position in the saddle if a good standard is to be attained later in more advanced work. Accuracy should come first; the other characteristics will come with practice.

Concentrated physical activity leads readily to fatigue which quickly results in the attention of both riders and horses deteriorating; it is of no benefit to work tired muscles. Rest periods during the ride such as walking on a loose rein, exercises at the halt and short discussions with riders dismounted are most beneficial.

(iv) Running through all riding instruction the factor of the safety of both rider and horse has constantly to be kept in mind. From the start pupils must be taught how to approach and handle a horse; kickers must be kept behind in a Ride or away from other horses. Beginners must not be allowed to go at a faster pace until they are secure at a slower one. They must be kept under close control. Galloping can be dangerous to a beginner with an insecure seat or an excitable or hard-mouthed horse.

When Jumping it is wise to follow a regular procedure such as that recommended in the chapter on this subject. Start with poles on the ground and follow with cavalletti at the lowest height; only when beginners are confident and able to follow the movement of the horse should the height be increased.

(v) It is important for those who teach to gain the confidence of their pupils and to establish an easy relationship straight away. The Instructor must find out their names, what tests they have done, whether they are riding their own horses or ponies and encourage them to talk. He must try and realise what sort of person he is dealing with and appreciate what his or her immediate problem may be. Is he dealing with an over-confident individual who knows it all or with a frightened, timid person?

Each must be treated differently; each is an individual with his own feelings; pupils have come for different reasons but mostly because they want to. The Instructor hopes they will go away saying "That was super! May we come again?"

With a frightened person the aim is to make him realise that he will not be asked to do anything that is beyond his capabilities or that he does not want to do. Having achieved this measure of confidence the Instructor must make him feel that his difficulties are understood but that no one else is aware that he is frightened.

Particularly when dealing with children an Instructor should use much tact and be sympathetic, giving the impression that he is "on their side" and out to help, not criticise. It is better to say "I think you would be more comfortable with your leathers a hole shorter" than "Your leathers are too long; shorten them!"

(vi) Group Instruction

In the earlier stages and when an Instructor is confronted with a number of pupils, it will be necessary to assemble them in Rides for instruction in groups. With a limited number of instructors available this becomes inevitable; people with insufficient ability to ride alone must be under supervision; they may be unable to control their horses sufficiently to be on their own. Moreover they will enjoy riding with others and carrying out the various movements.

But with group instruction there is always the prospect of boredom to contend with—too much attention to one pupil at the expense of others, too much hanging about, too much riding round and round on the same track, too much repetition, too much of the same voice. Every effort must be made to keep the class gay and happy, amused and interested.

With improvement and progress time should be allotted to supervised practice. There may be plenty of opportunities for practice at home but immediately after a new movement has been undertaken expert supervision is most necessary. Bad habits are established just as readily as good so that their prevention or elimination in the early stages is essential. It is much more difficult to teach a person who has acquired bad habits than somebody who has no preconceived ideas.

(vii) The Task System

When Pony Club members have passed their "B" Test and others have reached a similar standard, they should have the ability and enthusiasm to assimilate more advanced instruction. Here warning must again be sounded that riding must be enjoyable. Not everybody rides for the sake of riding nor aspires to great heights in equitation. Many ride as a means of indulging in a sport or game.

At this stage the teaching will be more individual and specialised, whether in the school or outside. It is improbable that all riders and horses will have reached the same standard; each has some special weakness he wishes to overcome or movements he hoped to improve. The Task System lends itself to teaching under such conditions; the procedure is as follows:

The members of the Ride are spaced out round the school as far apart as numbers allow. A rider catching up the horse next ahead will circle or turn across the school and rejoin the Ride in a vacant space. The Instructor should change the rein at regular intervals; Riders should pass right hand to right hand.

With a small Ride each rider may practice a different movement; with a larger number it may be necessary for all to do the same exercise. A demonstration may be very helpful. Each rider will then carry on in his own time while the Instructor looks on, criticises and advises, calling in individuals as necessary.

Riders at this stage must be encouraged to work things out for themselves, learning by trial and error and trial and success how they can produce the best results in their horses and in their own positions.

"Things we have to do we can only learn by doing".

This is the opportunity for the trained and experienced teacher with keen observation; he will see where the rider's—and the horse's—difficulties lie and be able to make helpful suggestions. This is the time for penetrating analysis expressed in a few, pointed and concise sentences. It is the feeling of the right movement and the right moment which the rider must achieve; in time this becomes habitual.

Skill is an efficient pattern of thought and movement, executed in the best way with the minimum of effort.

7. VOICE PRODUCTION

This is a subject which must be continually in the mind of anybody who aspires to teach. Out of doors an Instructor is faced with the wind, with aircraft and various mechanical noises; indoors he may have bad acoustics and echoes as well as external noises. So he must be prepared to alter his voice, in volume, pitch and tone, to meet different conditions.

Voice production is a highly technical matter. Correct breathing, the use of the throat and mouth, resonance, pitch, tone and volume must all be studied. The rate of speaking can be vital; the larger the audience and the worse the acoustics, the slower the rate of speech should be; in any case it should never be faster than the listener can absorb; pauses will be necessary for the same reason.

A speaker who is having difficulty in making himself heard must consider what the reason may be and change his delivery accordingly. Generally the first change should be to speak more slowly and more quietly, especially if the audience is coughing. Often a loud and jarring note makes an audience restless and noisy whereas a quiet, gentle tone causes them to concentrate, keep quiet and listen. Next lower the pitch. It may be necessary to increase the volume but never to shout. It does not pay to shout against extraneous noises—it is better to wait for them to pass or be stopped. It is worth reminding less experienced speakers always to face their audience; if they turn their backs and speak into a blackboard or the subject of a demonstration they must not be surprised if they are not heard.

II. TAKING A RIDE

1. INTRODUCTION

It is essential for an Instructor when teaching a number of pupils together, to be able to control them in a manege. It is not difficult and is largely a matter of practice. Moreover, handling a Ride well gives the Instructor great confidence in dealing with a class of pupils.

When drilling a Ride in a manege the movements cannot be properly carried out unless distances and intervals are maintained correctly and the paces are correct and even.

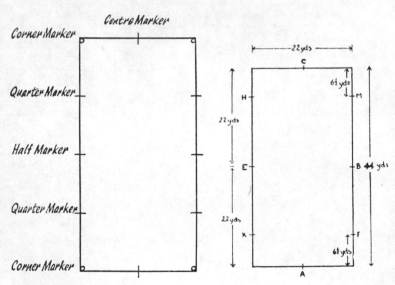

FIG. 1. A MANEGE WITH MARKERS

FIG. 2. A MANEGE MARKED OUT WITH LETTERED MARKERS

The manege must be laid out on as even ground as possible. A good size is 44 yds. by 22 yds., or, if a bigger size is required, 66yds. by 22 yds.

There should be a marker at each corner, and also half markers (half way along both long sides), centre markers (half way along the short sides) and quarter markers (quarter way along the long sides). See Figure 1. Lettered markers are not essential but are of great assistance to the Instructor. If used they should correspond with the lettering used for all official dressage competitions. (See Figure 2).

2. TERMS AND EXPRESSIONS USED IN THE MANEGE

The Instructor should make sure that the ride is familiar with any terms and words of command he or she proposes to use during the course of the lesson.

Pace. The pace of each member of the Ride should remain constant until commanded otherwise by the instructor. Any irregularity of pace or speed by one member of a Ride affects all those behind.

Distance. The correct distance between horses for most school work is approximately four ft., (i.e. half a horse's length). Each member of the Ride is responsible for keeping the correct distance from the horse in front. The Instructor should specify any different distance he may require for special purposes.

Correcting Distances. Unless told otherwise by the Instructor, for some particular purpose, a rider who has lost distance should automatically correct this, when approaching the short end of the manege, by making his turn before reaching the corner. The rest of the Ride should follow.

Dressing means keeping in line, or in position, during any movement. "Dressing by the left" means that the rider glances to his left and keeps in line with the rider at the left-hand end of the line. Each rider is responsible for keeping his own dressing. Unless commanded otherwise, dressing is always by the flank to which the turn is made.

The Track means the course the rider takes when riding round the manege, normally just inside the markers. The Ride always remains on the outside track unless otherwise ordered.

OUTSIDE TRACK. INSIDE TRACK. These terms may be used when required. The Outside Track is just inside the markers. The Inside Track is about five ft. inside the markers.

Going Large means that the rider rejoins the outside track after performing some movement, and continues round the manege in the track.

Leading File means the rider who is in the front of the ride and who is responsible for setting and maintaining the pace.

Rear File means the rider who is at the back of the ride.

Right Rein. Left Rein. A rider is on the Right Rein when moving in a right-handed (clockwise) direction, and on the Left Rein when moving in a left-handed (anti-clockwise) direction. Unless otherwise instructed, the ride remains on the same rein throughout an exercise.

Changing the Rein means changing direction. There are numerous methods of changing the rein— see"School Movements" on page 27. It is a mistake to get into the habit of changing the rein only by inclining across the school and it adds variety to change the rein by, for instance, turning across the school (single file, in rides or as a whole ride) or circling, or turning down the centre and going away in the opposite direction.

Numbering means each member of the Ride calling out his number.

WORDS OF COMMAND: *"Ride from the front—number"*, or, if preferred: *"Ride from the front—tell off by fours"* or *"threes"*.

The leading file turns his head to the inside and says, *"One"*, whereupon the rider behind him turns his head and says, *"Two"*, the next *"Three"*, and so on, to the back of the ride.

When "Telling off by Fours", the numbering goes, *"One, Two, Three, Four, One, Two, Three, Four"*, etc.

Dividing into Rides means dividing the class, after numbering, into equal groups for the purpose of performing School Movements.

WORDS OF COMMAND: *"Numbers one to four are number one ride. Numbers five to eight are number two ride"*, etc.

Or, if "Telling off by Fours", indicate each four and say : *"You are the first four. You are the second four"*, etc.

Proving means each rider indicating which Ride he is in. The instructor normally asks the class to "prove" after numbering and dividing them into rides.

WORDS OF COMMAND: *"Number one ride (or first four)—prove"*. *"Number two ride (or second four)—prove"*, etc.

On the word *"prove"*, each member of number (two or three) ride transfers his reins and stick to the outside hand and raises the inside arm straight forward, level with the shoulder, the hand flat with the thumb uppermost.

WORDS OF COMMAND: *"As you were"*.

The riders lower their arms and take up the reins in both hands, as before.

In Single File means the whole Ride follow one behind the other in the track of the leading file (N.B., the Ride remains in single file at all times unless commanded otherwise).

WORDS OF COMMAND : (for performing some such exercise as "Turning across the School"), *"Turning across the school in single file, leading file right—turn".*

The Leading File acts on the word *"turn"*.   The remainder of the Ride follow and turn when reaching the same spot.

In Succession means the riders are ordered to perform an exercise one at a time, starting normally with the leading file.

WORDS OF COMMAND : (for performing an exercise such as trotting and taking the rear of the ride), *"Leading files in succession trot and take the rear of the ride.   Number one—commence.   Next— next".*

In Rides means all members of the ride, on command, perform an exercise simultaneously.

WORDS OF COMMAND : (for performing an exercise such as 'Turning across the School"), *"Turning across the school in rides. Number one ride—left—turn."*

On the word *"turn"*, each member of number one ride turns off the track simultaneously and, on reaching the track on the opposite side of the manege, continues in single file, going large.

Whole Ride means each member of the whole class, on command, performs an exercise simultaneously.

WORDS OF COMMAND : (for performing an exercise such as "Turning across the School"), *"Turning across the school, whole ride—left—turn."*

Double Ride means the Ride being divided into two halves, each half then performing as a separate ride.

Forming a Double Ride.

WORDS OF COMMAND : *"Leading file down the centre."*

The leading file, followed by the remainder of the ride, turn down the centre and ride in a straight line.   As the leading file approaches the short end, the instructor gives the command, *"Odd numbers to the right, even numbers to the left—form a double ride."*

Two Rides are now formed, and from then on, on all occasions pass one another with right hand to right hand. Each rider closes up to four feet distance, and the ride on the left rein will be half a length behind the corresponding numbers in the other ride. When working with a Double Ride, it is essential that the two Leading Files should maintain the same, regular pace, and take their dressing from each other when riding down the long sides. The leading file of the Ride on the right rein is responsible for setting the pace, the leader on the left rein for keeping the dressing.

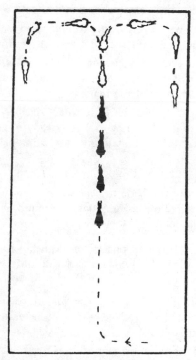

FIG. 3. FORMING A DOUBLE RIDE

3. WORDS OF COMMAND

There are two types of command: the "Preliminary" command which prepares the rider for what is to come, and the "Executive" command, upon which the rider acts.

> e.g., Preliminary Command: *"Prepare to trot."*
>
> Executive Command: *"Ride ter-rot."*

Give all words of command clearly, unhurriedly and in good time.

Start the preliminary warning well before the movement is to be begun. Allow a pause before giving the executive command.

Carefully judge the timing of the command on which the Ride or individual is to act, and give it clearly and with emphasis.

Take care that the timing is such that there is room for each member of the Ride to carry out the required movement. (e.g., not too near the corners of the manege).

If the Instructor wishes the Ride to act sharply, he will give a sharp word of command. If he wishes a steady and even transition from one pace to another, he will give a warning prior to a drawn-out command.

Words of command should only be given sufficiently loudly to enable everybody in the Ride to hear without undue effort. They should not be bawled out as on a parade ground.

The reasons are :

1. Horses and ponies very quickly learn to act on a word of command and will anticipate the rider's aids.

2. Pupils will ride more smoothly and keep alert if they have to concentrate on listening to the words of command.

When the ride is on the move it is better that the Instructor should make criticisms as the riders are coming towards him.

When addressing an individual the remarks should be preceded by the individual's name, e.g. *"Eve—shorten your reins"*, not *"Shorten your reins—Eve"*.

When asking a question first state the question, then name the person who is to answer.

Explaining the Movement.

When instructing riders for the first time—e.g., if the class is strange or if new riders have joined it, make quite sure that everyone understands the commands you propose to give and when they should act.

> e.g., *"I shall say, 'Ride—Walk—March' and on the word 'March', not before, I want each of you to make your pony walk on promptly and smoothly."*

Explain any unfamiliar exercise carefully and clearly. If in any doubt whether any member of the ride understands, demonstrate the movement while at the same time giving the appropriate words of command.

4. HINTS ON TAKING A RIDE

The Instructor is at all times responsible for the safety of his ride; therefore he must:

(*a*) Inspect the Ride for the safety of saddlery, in particular the stitching of girths, stirrup leathers and bridles; tightness of girths and fitting of bits. Shoeing. Ride standing still. Every effort should be made to reduce the time spent on inspection to a minimum.

(*b*) Find out if there are any kickers and place them at the rear of the ride. Warn others not to close up on them or to get closer than half a length to any animal.

New drill movements should be carried out at a walk before attempting any faster pace.

Until certain that the whole Ride understands the movement required and can carry it out, no attempt should be made to correct individual faults or raggedness.

Select an intelligent and capable leading file and rear file for each ride.

All periods should finish with an exercise that the Instructor knows will be performed well, i.e.,FINISH ON A GOOD NOTE.

If riders get out of place the Instructor should halt the Ride and sort it out quietly by command. He should keep control and not allow argument.

The command for turns and circles performed in Rides should be given so that the leading file of each Ride starts the movement in the same place.

Circles on to the centre. Give the command when the members of the Ride are going away from you, so that they circle and ride down the centre line straight towards you.

Movements in Rides. When doing Turns **without** a change of rein and circles **with** a change of rein, it is necessary to carry out the exercise twice if the rides are to finish up in their original order, otherwise they will be "back to front" (number four in the lead and number one at the rear).

Movements in Single File. Make sure the leading file knows, and is capable of carrying out, exactly what you want at a smooth, regular pace.

Drill Movements. It is wise for an inexperienced Instructor not to be too ambitious and to keep to the simplest movements at slow paces, avoiding the more complicated until he has gained confidence and experience.

This does not mean that the Ride must be dull and monotonous going round and round with no change of pace or movement. The Instructor must change the rein frequently by simple movements following the leading file and using a different method each time. (See Figures 7, 10 and 12.) These movements will entail both turns and circles (see also Figures 11 and 23) and will give the Instructor ample opportunity to insist on correct movements by the horse and the proper application of aids by the rider. There must also be frequent changes of pace. To practise control and to give the instructor a better opportunity for individual instruction, exercises performed individually by successive leading files may be employed (see Figure 24).

The above movements are as much as many beginners can manage.

As instructors gain experience and confidence they may attempt turns by fours across the school and so on to the more complicated movements.

Spotting Faults. It is important for the inexperienced Instructor to develop his powers of observation and to detect errors. This is vital if he is to become helpful to his pupils. Many riders have some fundamental fault which is impeding their progress and it is this which the Instructor must discover. To cultivate this art an Instructor must be clear in his own mind what he is looking for. At the trot, for example, is it the aids for increase of pace, the rider's position, the movement of the hands, the diagonal or the smoothness and rhythm of the horse's action? Unless he is experienced he must make up his mind which particular point or points he is looking for. He will then have a better chance of seeing the errors as they occur and of correcting them.

Procedure

In practice the taking of a Ride follows a sequence which begins with the inspection for safety and turnout.

There follows a period of walking and trotting round the manege on both reins to get settled down, warmed up, to adjust leathers and to allow the Instructor to assess the horses and riders.

Unless the Ride is part of a course, e.g.,in camp, the Instructor will then decide how to adapt his prepared programme. He will also be influenced by the conditions, the weather, school or open manege, the state of the ground and so on. The programme for a hot August day with hard going will be very different from that for a March day, with a cold east wind and the ground wet and holding.

The experienced Instructor will know just what to do next but the less experienced may lack such assurance. A knowledge of the Syllabus at the end of this book will help him.

5. MOUNTING AND DISMOUNTING BY NUMBERS

Mounting.

WORDS OF COMMAND : *"Ride—prepare to mount"*. Each rider takes up his reins and stick correctly and positions himself ready to place the foot in the stirrup iron. (Note : The Army drill is not adhered to here, because of the variation in size of riders and ponies.)

"*One*".   Having placed the foot in the iron, each rider takes the waist or front of the saddle with the hand not holding the reins and stick, springs up and stands upright on the stirrup irons. facing across the pony's back.

"*Two*".   Each rider passes his leg over the pony's back and settles lightly in the saddle, facing the pony's head.

"*Three*".   Each rider takes the stirrups, reins and stick and sits up in the ordinary riding position.

Dismounting.

WORDS OF COMMAND: "*Ride—prepare to dismount*".   Each rider quits both stirrups and places his hands on the pony's withers.

"*Dismount*".   Each rider swings the body forward, keeping the weight central along the pony's back, brings both legs up behind and above the pony's back and then vaults off and lands with the feet together in line with the pony's forelegs.   He stands straight facing the same direction as the pony and holds the reins close to the bit with the hand nearest the pony, the other hand holding the end of the reins.

6.   PHYSICAL EXERCISES

It is, very often, a good plan to start a ride with some of the physical exercises referred to in "The Manual of Horsemanship". When doing these exercises, it is essential to get the ride going at a steady, even pace and well closed up.   The exercises may also be performed, with other variations, at the halt.

For exercises requiring that the hands are taken off the reins, the reins may be knotted.   For such exercises, the leading file should keep his reins and not perform the exercise.

Riding without Stirrups.

This is an excellent method of getting the riders down into their saddles, but periods of riding without stirrups at the trot should be short, to avoid the risk of over-straining the muscles. If the rider holds the front arch of the saddle lightly he is better able to maintain the correct position and will find the exercise less tiring. The pace should be slow and even.

WORDS OF COMMAND: *"Ride, quit your stirrups. Cross your stirrups."* Then, *"Ride, take your stirrups."*

Note. It is considered that the rising trot without stirrups is too severe an exercise for children who only ride occasionally.

Rising and sitting down at the trot, with stirrups.

WORDS OF COMMAND: *"Ride, commence rising"* and, *"Ride, cease rising."*

Touching the Toes.

The Ride should be allowed to control their horses with the outside hand. The exercise may be performed either with or without stirrups.

WORDS OF COMMAND: (In this case when the Ride are on the left rein); *"All reins in the right hand. Left hand hanging down."* The word, *"down"* is given sharply. The left hand should hang down behind the thigh. Then, *"Touching the left toe. Ride— one-(down)—two-(up). One—two—one—two."*

It should be remembered that it is the coming up that really does the good in this exercise and this should therefore be performed as quickly as possible. For this reason, the words, *"Two-up"* should be given sharply. The leg must be kept in the correct position throughout and not drawn up to meet the hand.

Change the rein for touching the right toe.

Body Bending Forwards and Backwards.

Words of Command: Preliminary Command: *"Body bending forwards and backwards."* Then, *"O-n-e—forwards."* The body should bend slightly forwards from the waist, head up and eyes looking between the pony's ears. Then, *"T-w-o—upright."* Then, *"T-h-r-e-e—right back."*

The rider should allow the body to go back until the shoulders are touching the horse's croup. The head should be up and the eyes looking at the horse's head. Under no circumstances should the rider be kept in this position for more than a few seconds. Then, *"F-o-u-r—upright."*

7. SCHOOL MOVEMENTS

Throughout the lesson, the ride automatically remains :

In Single File
On the Track
On the Same Rein } Until otherwise instructed.
At the Same Pace
At the Same Distance

At the discretion of the Instructor, the following may also be carried out automatically :

Rising Trot—Sitting Trot. The Rising Trot should be used when going large round the track and the Sitting Trot when performing any school movement which involves turning or circling off the track.

Trotting on a Diagonal (Rising Trot). A Ride should change the diagonal on which they are trotting, with each change of rein, e.g., riding on the right diagonal when on the left rein and on the left diagonal when on the right rein.

Holding the Stick. Change the stick into the other hand with each change of rein.

When training a horse this may not always be expedient, expecially during the period when a change of bend is being sought.

Most exercises may be performed by the Ride in five different ways :

In Single File.
In Succession (i.e. individually).
In Rides.
Whole Ride.
Double Ride.

The following are the basic school movements.   They are not the only ones and may be enlarged upon by an ingenious Instructor with an intelligent class.

Movements from the Halt.

From the halt, the rider will only move on the word, "*march.*" (For turns and changes of pace on the move, the word "*march*" is unnecessary.)

WORDS OF COMMAND :
"*Ride—walk—march.*"
"*Ride—rein-back—march.*"
"*Ride—right turn—march.*"
"*Ride—turn on the forehand.   Right turn—march.*"

Movements on the Move.

A PRELIMINARY COMMAND: "*Prepare to—*" or "*To the—*" is often advisable, and for the canter is essential.

EXECUTIVE COMMAND:
"*Ride—ter-rot.*"
"*Ride—w-a-a-l-k.*"
"*Ride—canter-r-r.*"
"*Ride—h-a-l-t.*"

To address the Ride at the Halt.

There are two methods, depending on whether the Instructor wishes the members of the Ride to maintain their normal distances, or to close up.

1. To halt the ride—maintaining distances.

Give the command : *"Prepare to halt, Ride—Halt."*
If it is desired to change direction, this may be followed by :
"Right turn (or left, inwards, outwards turn)—march."
(See Figure 4.)

2. Closing up to Halt in line.

(a) When maintaining the direction, the command is :
"Ride to the halt—on the left (or right) form a Ride".

On completion of the command, the Leading File halts. The remainder of the ride incline to the side ordered and form up in line with 1 ft. distances between riders' knees. (See Figure 5a.)

(b) When altering the direction, the command is : *"Leading file right (or left) turn. Ride to the halt on the left (or right) form a Ride."* (See Figure 5b.)

Moving off from the Halt.

1. When distances have been maintained at the halt,
each rider has room to turn if required. Therefore the commands may be :

(a) *"Whole ride—walk march."* in which case each rider moves straight forward and if not already on the track, obeys the normal drill procedure on reaching the track, (e.g. *"Go large on the left (right) rein"*).

(b) *"Whole ride right (or left) turn—march."* Then, when the turn is completed : *"Ride, walk—march."*

(c) *"Whole ride right (or left) turn and walk—march, on the left (or right) rein."*

2. **When distances have been closed up.**

If maintaining direction, give the command : "*In single file from the right (or left) walk—march.*" The leading File moves straight forward. The remainder move forward and incline on to the track of the Leading File (See Figure 6).

If altering direction, give the command : "*In single file to the left (or right) Leading File left (or right) turn, walk— march.*" The Leading File moves forward, turning as ordered. The remainder move off in succession, following the Leading File.

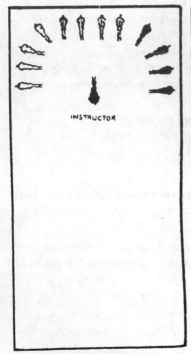

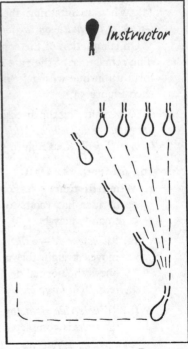

FIG. 4. RIDE HALTED—
MAINTAINING DISTANCES

FIG. 5(a). FORMING A RIDE—
MAINTAINING DIRECTION

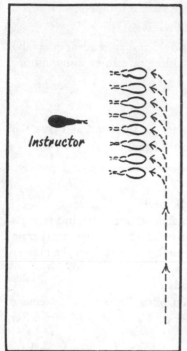

FIG. 5(b). FORMING A RIDE—
CHANGING DIRECTION

FIG. 6. MOVING OFF IN SINGLE
FILE AFTER FORMING A RIDE

"Walk on a loose rein."

The rider lengthens his reins, allowing the horse to stretch its head and neck as far as it wishes. The pace of the walk should not be allowed to slacken and the rider must be ready to correct any deviation from the track.

The walk on a loose rein may be used after any strenuous exercise in order to allow both horse and rider to relax.

"Sit at ease."

The rider lengthens the reins and relaxes.

The Instructor should allow the ride to rest at frequent intervals, either by walking on a loose rein, sitting at ease or dismounting, while he talks to them.

"Make much of your Horses."

The rider places reins and stick in the left hand and pats the horse's neck three times with the right hand.

INCLINES.

(a) **"Inclining across the School"**

The rein is changed by inclining diagonally, in a straight line, across the manege, from the first quarter marker on one long side, to the last quarter marker on the other.

Methods :

(i) **In Single File.** WORDS OF COMMAND: *"Inclining across the school in single file—leading file—right (or left)—incline."*

On the word *"incline"*, the leading file moves off the track. The rear files follow in single file and start the movement at the same spot as the leading file (see Figure 7).

(ii) **In Rides.** WORDS OF COMMAND: *"Inclining across the school in rides. Number one ride—right (or left)—incline."*

On the word *"incline"*, each member of Number One Ride moves simultaneously off the track. The dressing should be taken by the leading file. The riders' shoulders should be in line (see Figure 8).

(iii) **Whole Ride.** Only possible if the length of the manege and the number of riders permit.

Substitute the words *"whole ride"* for *"in rides."*

(iv) **Double Ride.** Only possible if the Ride is opened out and distances are maintained accurately (see page 19 *re* closing up). WORDS OF COMMAND : *"Inclining across the school in single file—leading files—inwards incline."*

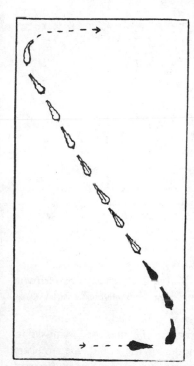

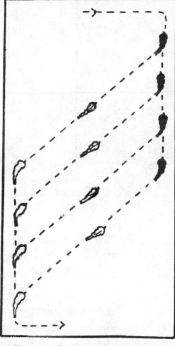

FIG. 7. INCLINING ACROSS THE SCHOOL IN SINGLE FILE

FIG. 8. INCLINING ACROSS THE SCHOOL IN RIDES

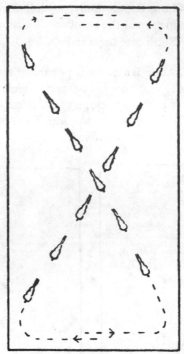

FIG. 9.   DOUBLE RIDE—LEADING FILES, INWARDS INCLINE

(b)   **"Large Figure-of-Eight."**

WORDS OF COMMAND: *"Large figure-of-eight by inclining across the school.   In single file—commence."*

On the word *"commence"*, the leading file moves off the track and inclines across the manege, followed in single file by the remainder of the Ride; then repeats the movement from the first quarter marker on the next long side.

The exercise continues until the order, "*Ride—go large*" is given.

Note. If the word "*commence*" is used to start any movement, the Ride will continue to execute the movement until told to "*go large.*"

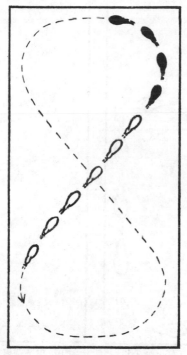

FIG. 10.   LARGE FIGURE-OF-EIGHT

TURNS.

(a) "Turning across the School."

The rider makes a right-angled turn (90 degrees) off the track and rides in a straight line across the manege, turning the same way on reaching the track on the opposite side.

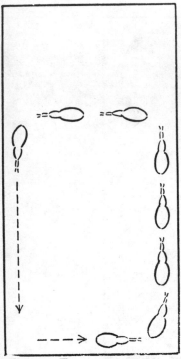

FIG. 11.   TURNING ACROSS THE SCHOOL IN SINGLE FILE

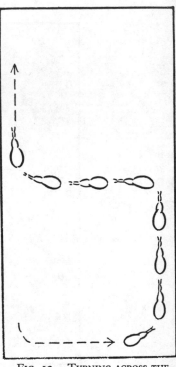

FIG. 12.   TURNING ACROSS THE SCHOOL AND CHANGING THE REIN IN SINGLE FILE

Methods :

(i) **In Single File.** WORDS OF COMMAND: *"Turning across the school in single file—leading file right (or left)—turn."* (See Figure 11.)

(ii) **In Rides.** WORDS OF COMMAND: *"Turning across the school in rides—number one ride, right (or left)—turn."* (See Figure 13.)

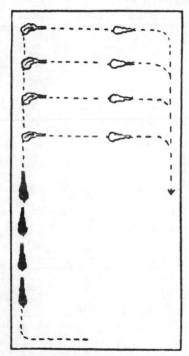

FIG. 13. TURNING ACROSS THE SCHOOL IN RIDES

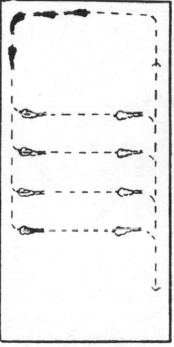

FIG. 14. TURNING ACROSS THE SCHOOL AND CHANGING THE REIN IN RIDES

On the word "*turn*", each member of the ride turns off the track simultaneously. The dressing should be by the rider on the left, when turning to the left, and vice versa. The riders' shoulders should be in a straight line, parallel with the long sides of the manege. On reaching the track, the riders turn again, in the same direction and "go large" in single file.

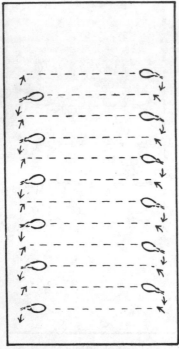

FIG. 15.   DOUBLE RIDE—RIDES
INWARD TURN

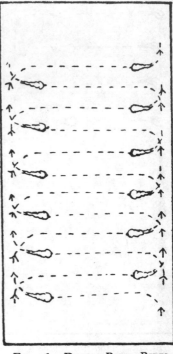

FIG. 16.   DOUBLE RIDE—RIDES
INWARDS TURN AND CHANGE

Each Ride should be turned at the same place in the manege.

(iii) **Whole Ride.** As above, substituting the words, *"whole ride."*

(iv) **Double Ride.** The words of command should be timed, so that the turn is made when the rides are on opposite sides of the manege.

WORDS OF COMMAND: *"Turning across the school —rides, inwards—turn."*

The members of each Ride turn off the track simultaneously and the Rides should pass each other in the centre, passing right hand to right hand. (See Figure 15.)

(b) **"Turning across the School and changing the rein."**

This exercise may also be performed in single file, in rides, whole ride, and double ride.

WORDS OF COMMAND: The Preliminary command, in each case, is: *"Turning across the School and changing the rein,"* followed by Executive command: *"Leading file (number one ride or whole ride) left (or right) turn—and change."*

The rider changes direction when reaching the track on the opposite side of the manege, (i.e., instead of turning left and then left again, he first turns left and then turns right). (See Figure 12.)

(c) **"Turning down the Centre Line."**

At the short end of the manege, the rider makes a right-angled turn off the track and rides in a straight line to the other end. He halts just off the track and waits for the rest of the ride to pass, joining in as the rear file, and going large.

This exercise may be used as a school movement, and also to practise trotting or cantering over a low pole, which could be placed in the centre of the manege.

Methods:

(i) **In Succession.** WORDS OF COMMAND: "*Leading files in succession, down the centre, halt, and join the rear of the ride—commence.*"

Each rider, as he becomes the leading file, turns down the centre automatically on reaching the next centre marker, until every member of the Ride has performed the exercise.

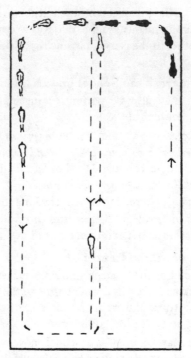

FIG. 17.   LEADING FILES IN SUCCESSION DOWN THE CENTRE

(ii) **In Rides.** WORDS OF COMMAND: *"Rides in succession down the centre, halt and join the rear. Number One Ride—commence."*

The members of Number One Ride turn off the track simultaneously and proceed in line abreast, going large at the rear of the remainder of the ride, in single file.

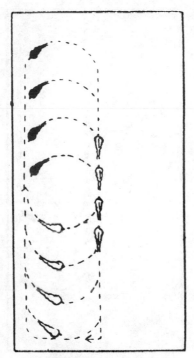

FIG. 18. CIRCLING ON TO THE CENTRE LINE IN RIDES

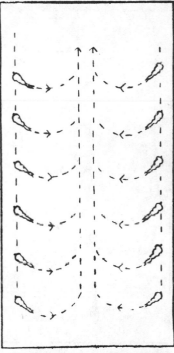

FIG. 19. DOUBLE RIDE—RIDES CIRCLE ON TO THE CENTRE LINE

CIRCLING.

The Preliminary commands, in each case, are as in the headings given below.

   (a) **"Circle on to the Centre line and return to track"** (in single file, in Rides, whole Ride, double Ride).

      EXECUTIVE COMMAND: *"Leading file (Number One Ride, Ride, Rides)—circle."*

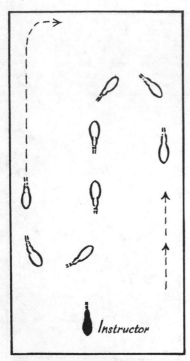

FIG. 20. HALF FIGURE-OF-EIGHT IN SINGLE FILE

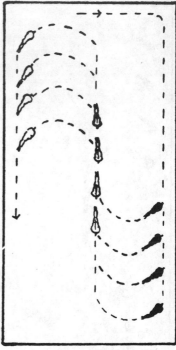

FIG. 21. HALF FIGURE-OF-EIGHT IN RIDES

On the word *"circle"* the rider describes a semicircle on to an imaginary centre line (between the two centre markers), then proceeds to ride in a straight line towards the centre marker until given the command, *"Away."*

The rider then describes another semicircle back on to the track and goes large (on the same rein). (See Figures 18 and 19.)

(b) **"Half Figure-of-Eight**—(In single file, in Rides, whole Ride)."

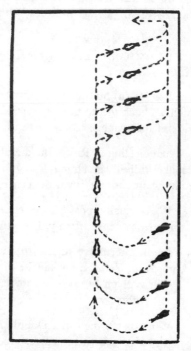

FIG. 22. CIRCLING ON TO THE CENTRE LINE AND INCLINING BACK TO THE TRACK

EXECUTIVE COMMAND: *"Leading file (Number One Ride, Ride)—half figure of eight."*

Proceed as for (a), but on the command, *"Away"*, the rider makes a semicircle back to the track on the opposite side, going large on the other rein, (i.e., he first circles right and then circles left). (See Figures 20 and 21.)

(c) **"Circle on to the Centre line and incline back to the track**—(in single file, in Rides, Whole Ride, Double Ride)."

EXECUTIVE COMMAND: *"Leading file (Number One Ride, Ride, Rides)—circle."*

Proceed as for (a) but on the command, *"Away"*, the rider inclines back to the track in a straight line, on the same side of the manege, going large on the other rein.

N.B. When circling in Rides, the members of the rides make individual semicircles, but fall into single file when coming down the centre line.

It is usually possible to circle two or even three rides consecutively, from the same spot.

As an alternative to the Instructor giving the command, *"Away,"* it can be arranged that the signal is given by a nod from the Leading File of the ride.

When performed in a Double Ride, each rider makes a pair with his corresponding number in the opposite ride, when coming down the centre line.

(d) "Individual Circles."

EXECUTIVE COMMAND: *"Numbers One—circle right (or left). Numbers Two—circle right (or left)"* and so on.

On the word *"right (or left),"* number one of each ride comes off the track and describes a small circle, judging it so that he rejoins the track at the rear of his ride (into the space vacated by the number one of the following ride.

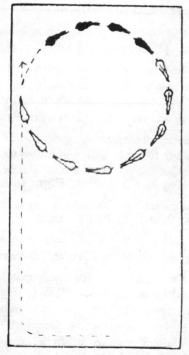

FIG. 23. LARGE CIRCLE, HALF THE SCHOOL, IN SINGLE FILE

(e) **"Circling in succession to take the rear."**

EXECUTIVE COMMAND: *"Leading file—circle—right (or left). Next—next—next"* and so on.

On the word *"right (or left),"* the leading file moves off the track and describes a large circle, judging it so that he rejoins the track at the rear of the whole Ride.

(f) **"Circling in Single File."**

Circles may be performed anywhere and be of any size, as required by the Instructor.

EXECUTIVE COMMAND: *"Large circle—half the school, in single file—leading file, circle"* or (*"leading file, commence"*).

On the word *"circle"* (or *"commence"*) the leading file, followed by the rest of the Ride in single file, describes a large circle taking up the whole width of the manege, rejoining the track at the same spot, and going large.

The exercise may be made *"continuous,"* the Ride continuing to circle until told to *"go large."*

(g) **"Circling in a Figure-of-Eight in Single File."**

This exercise is normally started at the centre marker (on the short side of the manege).

EXECUTIVE COMMAND: *"Large circles—half the school, leading file—circle"* or (*"leading file, commence"*).

On the word *"right"* (or *"commence"*), the leading file, followed by the rest of the Ride in single file, describes half a large circle, taking up the whole width of the manege, but when reaching the centre line, changes the rein and describes a second circle, completing the movement by circling back on to the track, rejoining it at the place at which the exercise was started.

EXERCISES PERFORMED INDIVIDUALLY IN SUCCESSION.

Variations of this exercise are numerous, and include some of the methods, given above.   Some other examples are given below.

(a)   **"Leading files in succession trot (or canter) and take the rear."**

EXECUTIVE COMMAND: *"Leading file—commence.   Next —next."*

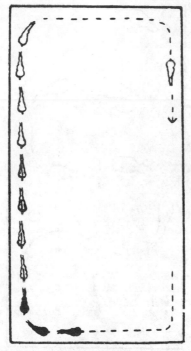

FIG. 24.   LEADING FILES IN SUCCESSION
TAKE THE REAR

(b)**"Rear files (or leading files) in succession, Ride as commanded."**

EXECUTIVE COMMAND: After the preliminary command, the Instructor may require the rider to, "*Trot to the next quarter marker, walk, halt, rein back two steps, forward at the trot,*" etc., etc.

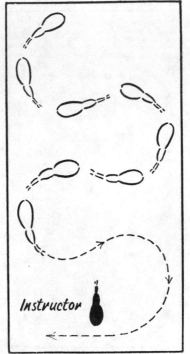

FIG. 25. SERPENTINE IN SINGLE FILE. FOUR
LARGE LOOPS ACROSS THE SCHOOL

LOOPS.

(a) **"Serpentine, Large Loops".**

WORDS OF COMMAND: *"Serpentine in single file, three (or four) large loops across the school—commence."*

On the word *"commence,"* the Leading File, followed by the rest of the Ride, describes large, regular loops down the whole length of the school, going as far as the track with each loop, starting at the short end and going large when reaching the other end. (See Figure 25.)

(b) **"Shallow loops down the long side".**

WORDS OF COMMAND: *"One loop (or two loops) in single file, down the long side—commence."*

On the word *"commence,"* the Leading File, followed by the rest of the Ride, describes one, or two (as directed) shallow loops down the long side, coming between two and five yards inside the track, and rejoining it at, or just beyond, the last quarter marker.

8. EXAMPLE OF A SIMPLE RIDE

THE INSTRUCTOR: *"Ride, from the front tell off by twos."*

THE RIDE: Number, *"one-two-one-two-one-two-one-two"* from front to rear.

THE INSTRUCTOR: *"Numbers one, prove."*

THE RIDE: Numbers one—Transfer the reins to the outside and raise the inside arm.

THE INSTRUCTOR: *"As you were."*

THE RIDE: Numbers one lower the inside arm.

THE INSTRUCTOR: *"Leading file, down the centre."*

THE RIDE: Leading file on reaching the centre marker, turns down the centre followed by the Ride.

THE INSTRUCTOR: *"Numbers one to the right, numbers two to the left—form a double Ride."*

THE RIDE: On reaching the opposite end each number one turns to the right: each number two to the left.

THE INSTRUCTOR: As leading files are half-way up the side of the manege—*"By twos, down the centre."*

THE RIDE: As each number one and two meet at the centre marker they turn as a pair down the centre.

THE INSTRUCTOR: *"First pair to the right, second pair to the left."*

THE RIDE: As pairs reach the opposite end of the manege they turn right and left alternately.

THE INSTRUCTOR: As leading pairs are half-way up the manege —*"By fours, down the centre."*

THE RIDE: As each pair reach the centre marker they turn as fours down the centre.

THE INSTRUCTOR: *"First four to the right, second four to the left."*

THE RIDE: Turn in fours.

THE INSTRUCTOR: *"By eights, down the centre."*

THE RIDE: Fours turn at top and advance down centre as eights.

THE INSTRUCTOR: *"Prepare to halt—Ride—halt."*

Then Unwind.

THE INSTRUCTOR: *"Ride—trot (walk or canter) march."*

THE RIDE: Obey.

THE INSTRUCTOR: *"Fours to the right and left."*

THE RIDE: At the end of the manege the four on the right turn right, the four on the left turn left at the bottom of the manege.

THE INSTRUCTOR: As fours are half-way up the side—"*By fours, down the centre.*"

THE RIDE: The four on the right rein precede the four on the left rein down the centre.

THE INSTRUCTOR: "*Pairs to right and left.*"

THE RIDE: Pairs turn as above.

THE INSTRUCTOR: "*By pairs down the centre.*"

THE RIDE: Obey.

THE INSTRUCTOR: "*Numbers one to the right, numbers two to the left.*"

THE RIDE: Obey.

THE INSTRUCTOR: "*By single file, down the centre form a single Ride.*"

THE RIDE: Obey.

THE INSTRUCTOR: "*Leading file, on the right (or left) rein.*"

THE RIDE: Follow the leading file.

THE INSTRUCTOR: When Ride are all on one side of the manege —"*Ride—right-turn and halt.*"

THE RIDE: Turn and halt in the centre.

THE INSTRUCTOR: "*Ride—sit at ease.*"

THE RIDE: Let out the reins and sit at ease.

The Instructor may then make some observations on the riding, if the ride was part of a lesson, demonstrating faults, praising liberally what was well done, and in every case ending up on "a good note."

III. INSTRUCTION IN JUMPING

What to teach.   The Instructor must know intimately the section "Jumping" in "The Manual of Horsemanship" in which the jumping position is clearly defined and illustrated, the construction of schooling fences shown and riding over fences and cavalletti explained.

The aim is to teach the rider to sit correctly over fences, to control his horse and so enable it to jump a fence with maximum ease, efficiency and enjoyment to both.

Certain facilities are necessary; the simplest and most effective to start with are a few thick poles and a set of four or six cavalletti. After these a few small, preferably solid, artificial jumps and some natural fences and ditches are necessary. An assistant is useful both to handle the jumps and to help with instruction. At all stages someone, who may be the Instructor or leading file, who can demonstrate is invaluable. (See demonstrations on pages 3 and 5).

Next the method of instruction has to be decided upon, bearing in mind the safety of pupils and the standard of riders and horses; this, for beginners, involves Group instruction in a Ride, with strict control.

They should keep their reins and ride their normal length (which will be on the short side at this stage anyway). It is best for them not to start jumping until they are secure at the trot and canter.

The Instructor, having seen the ride at these paces, will know which are the keen and which the "sticky" horses and will arrange for the free ones to go first; alternatively they may go individually before the others.

A single pole will be laid on the track of the manege and the Ride will walk over it, either spaced well apart or closed up as the Instructor sees fit. When all are walking quietly without breaking into a trot they may be permitted to trot and when all are trotting quietly a second pole may be added 18 ft. to 20 ft. away. Start walking over the two and when all will walk without breaking they may trot.

Cavalletti are best placed at the side of a school or beside a hedge or wall in the open. A wing is a help. A roped or fenced lane may be used but care must be taken that horses do not rush.

Once the horses are going well the riders may go individually or two together, following each other, and going round a few times rather than for only one turn.

As the lessons progress from the simple pole on the ground to a cavalletto, slightly higher, the horse will give a hop which will be the pupil's first jump; if secure at the canter he should have no difficulty in following the movement of the horse.

Lean forward, look forward, is enough to think about at this stage.

When a beginner is riding confidently over one cavalletti a second may be introduced but it should be placed one or two canter strides beyond the first.

Three cavalletti with a whole stride between each is enough for small children.

Later the procedure "Method of Use" for cavalletti on page 44 of "The Manual of Horsemanship" may be followed.

Cavalletti, with their varieties of height, width and spacing, can provide all necessary obstacles for the beginner for some time to come but monotony may be avoided and change enjoyed by allowing the young rider to trot over poles on the ground or at very low heights between the wings of a jumping course and over small ditches if available.

As soon as the horses are going freely enough for individual jumping, whether over a series of cavalletti or single fences, safety and control by the Instructor require some such drill described as follows:

DRILL FOR THE JUMPING LESSON

The following drill ensures law, order and safety when individual jumping instruction is being given. It is also beneficial as a means of impressing discipline upon horses, but if they are not going well it is better that the riders should not be restricted to a 20 yards run at a fence, but should keep going round.

Form the Ride up opposite and at right-angles to the jump, where all can get a clear view of the fence, the Instructor situated, if possible, facing the Ride on the opposite side to the fence, or with

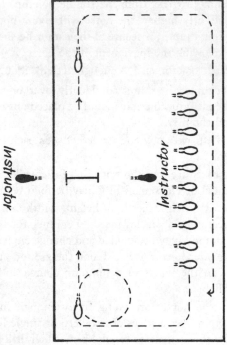

FIG. 26. A DRILL FOR A JUMPING LESSON

the back to the Ride if on the same side of the fence. On the command—"*No.* 1, *ready*"—No. 1 rides out and halts 20 yards from and facing the jump. On the command—"*Go*"—No. 1 goes over the fence, halts and stands still 20 yards beyond the fence, while at the same time No. 2 moves to the position vacated by No. 1 and halts.

On the command—"*Next go*"—No. 1 waits until joined by No. 2 and then returns to the rear of his original position in the Ride ; No. 2 passes over the jump to a position beside No. 1 and No. 3 moves to the position vacated by No. 2. (See Figure 26.)

"As an alternative, instead of coming out and halting, the next rider—or next two riders—may be brought out to circle quietly at a trot until called upon to jump. The importance of 'warming-up' before jumping must be stressed from the start".

The Instructor should insist on control of the horse after the jump; under no circumstances must it be allowed to rush back and rejoin the others—this is bad training and a frequent cause of falls.

The position of the Ride in relation to the jump is important and affects the performance. Normally well away to one side, as shown in the diagram, so that all can see each performance is a good position.

The Instructor is shown in one of several positions he can take up, but he must be able to see and be heard. Criticism is best made quietly after the jump.

With "sticky" horses or a strange looking fence the Ride is best placed on the landing side. A bad mistake, too often made, is to ask horses, half-asleep, to leave the Ride and jump a fence a few yards in front of them. On the other hand with a rushing horse this often has a calming effect.

Having, it is to be hoped, some schooling fences (as described in the Manual) available the Instructor will gradually come on to the stage described as Riding over Practice Jumps. Jumping may now be undertaken at all paces. It is wise, when there are a number of riders, to maintain control by following the same drill. As the seat improves and it becomes possible to lengthen the leathers for movements on the level, so it will be found advantageous to ride with shorter stirrups and to adopt the jumping position (as described in the Manual) over fences.

As riders progress, some faster than others, the Task System again comes into its own and there are practically no limits to its variation from riding over a single problem fence to a complete cross-country or show-jumping course.

The Instructor will continually have in mind two sections in the Manual—Common Causes of Bad Jumping and Refusals (page 49) and Rushing (page 52). The correction of these faults may well form the tasks for those riding older horses while young horses may follow the lines suggested under Jumping when Mounted (page 39) in "Training the Young Pony."

MORE ADVANCED JUMPING

When jumping natural obstacles the Instructor should be mounted and should demonstrate. A tantivy, cantering on over several obstacles, is of great benefit provided the Ride is well disciplined and spaced.

For the confident and more advanced riders variation can be introduced with advantage by:

    (a) Building awkward jumps and combinations of jumps,

    (b) Building jumps on the turn, at odd angles or on slopes,

    (c) Jumping without stirrups or reins,

    (d) Taking off hats, etc., over the jumps.

Note 1. Jumping without stirrups or saddles tends to develop false grip with the back of the knee and calf unless care is taken to prevent it.

Note 2. To get the most enjoyment out of jumping, riders must be able to get a good free jump from their horses. They need to be shown how to construct a fence with a clear-cut ground line, and to have it emphasised that in cold blood the horse should be 'introduced' to the jump and not over-faced.

It is a mistake to beat or chase a refusing horse over a fence. More often than not it is the rider who is at fault. It is better (*a*) to lower the fence, if it is movable, or to try a lower fence which the horse will jump; (*b*) to give the horse a lead from another horse; (*c*) to put up another rider.

See Common Causes of Bad Jumping and Refusals in the "Manual of Horsemanship."

THE USE OF CAVALLETTI

An explanation in detail of the use of cavalletti is given in both the "Manual of Horsemanship" and "Training the Young Pony". This is recommended as a most valuable method of training both rider and horse.

IV. SPECIAL CONSIDERATIONS FOR THE INSTRUCTION OF THE VERY YOUNG

1. Small children need a lot of attention and the Instructor can well do with two or three assistants.   These will be wanted to put the riders properly in the saddle, to adjust stirrups and saddlery, to help with lazy or awkward ponies, to give individual instruction and such like.

2. A small rider mounting a tall pony should lengthen the stirrup leather in order to reach the iron and to save prodding the pony with the toe, or stand on higher ground than the pony.

3. If the child's hands are too small to accommodate four reins comfortably, knot the bottom reins together and hold the top rein, or use a snaffle or single rein pelham.

4. A length of blind cord attached from the bit via the brow band, through the "D" on the front arch of the saddle and back via the brow band to the bit on the opposite side, acts as an over-head check and is invaluable on a pony that a child is unable to prevent from lowering its head.   The cord must be long enough to allow the pony to jump.

5. When checking to see that leathers are of equal length, make the pupil take the feet out of the stirrups and ensure that the saddle is straight on the pony's back, then stand in front to see that the leathers are of equal length.

6. The selection of a sensible child or an assistant Instructor on a free-going pony, to act as 'leading file' is essential.

7. Teaching the young gives much scope for initiative on the part of the Instructor.   First and foremost he must get their confidence; *next they must enjoy themselves and if they can be made to laugh the day is almost won.   They must never be bored.* If they spend most of the time playing games, especially if these are designed to incorporate lessons recently taught, and handling their ponies they will hardly realise that they are being taught.   Frequent changes and continuous occupation are the best antidotes to boredom ; the children should spend as much time as possible doing things themselves and not sitting about watching or listening to other people. RIDING ROUND AND ROUND A MANEGE SOON BECOMES EXCEEDINGLY DULL.

It is much easier for the Instructor to be dismounted.

8. Instructors must remember that boys up to the age of 15 may be more highly-strung and nervous than they will like to admit; a fall hurts their dignity, and they must not be made to look foolish in front of the Ride. Often they are a great challenge to the initiative, inspiration and ingenuity of their Instructor to maintain a high level of enthusiasm, especially in the putting over of Stable-Management sessions.

V. LITERATURE FOR INSTRUCTORS

"The Manual of Horsemanship" of the British Horse Society and the Pony Club is the textbook upon which all instruction should be based.

This book — "The Instructors' Handbook" — explains to instructors how to instruct. They should follow the sequence of instruction in Appendix X.

The system of riding and horse management as taught, is further explained in film strip lectures, films and booklets, a list of which is included in the Pony Club Year Book each year.

PONY CLUB PUBLICATIONS

STANDARD BOOKS OF REFERENCE FOR INSTRUCTORS

The Manual of Horsemanship ...   .

Training the Young Horse and Pony ...   .

Keeping a Pony at Grass by Mrs. O. Faudel-Phillips, F.I.H.   ...   ...

Mounted Games and Gymkhanas ...   .

Polo for the Pony Club ...   .

Camping for the Pony Club   ...   .

A Guide to the Purchase of Children's Ponies   ...   .

A Guide to Pony Trekking and Mounted Expeditions   ...   .

A Guide to Dress and Turnout for Members and Associates of the Pony Club   ...   .

Points of the Horse Chart   ...   .

Points of the Horse Game   ...   .

*Riding to Hounds   ...   .

Notes for Five-Minute Lectures—Foxhunting   ...   .

*Basic Training for Young Horses and Ponies by Col. and Mrs.
V.D.S.Williams   ...   .

*The Foot and Shoeing by Major C. Davenport, F.R.C.V.S.   ...   .

The General Purpose Seat by Col. The Hon. C.G.Cubitt, D.S.O., T.D.,
D.L., and Col. G.T.Hurrell, O.B.E.   ...   .

*Bits and Bitting by Col. The Hon. C.G.Cubitt   ...   .

*The Aids and Their Applications by Col. The Hon. C.G.Cubitt, D.S.O.,
T.D., D.L.   ...   .

(Film Strips are also available for each of these titles)

The Pony Club Standards of Efficiency   ...   .

The Pony Club Hunting and Country Lore Tests   ...   .

Rules for Dressage   ...   .

Rules for Combined Training   ...   .

The Competitors' Guide   ...   .

*Quiz Questions for the Pony Club   ...   .

Individual Test Sheets ('D', 'C', 'B', and 'A' Standards)   ...   .

*Riding by Mrs. V.D.S. Williams *(Published for the British Horse Society
by Educational Productions Ltd.)* ...   .

An up-to-date list of publications is shown in the Pony Club
Year Book, issued annually. A list of books recommended for further reading is maintained by the B.H.S.

* These are available from
          BARRON'S 113 Crossways Pk. Dr., Woodbury, N.Y. 11797

Publications issued annually

The Pony Club Horse Trials

The Pony Club Year Book (containing the Rules and the "Administrative Notes")

Prince Philip Cup—Mounted Games Championship—Rules

These and other publications connected with the horse are available from

THE BRITISH HORSE SOCIETY
National Equestrian Centre, Kenilworth
Warwickshire, CV8 2LR

* These are available from

BARRON'S
113 Crossways Park Drive
Woodbury, New York 11797

FILM STRIP LECTURES

The principle of the film strip is the same as that of the colour slide, except that the pictures are in a continuous strip instead of in separate slides. A special 35 mm. film strip projector is required and an ordinary cinematograph screen. These may be hired from photographic stores, schools, etc., or an attachment to hold the strips can be fitted to many types of 35 mm. slide projectors.

There is a printed lecture to accompany each strip, but the lecturer is advised to prepare the talk thoroughly beforehand so as to avoid reading from the script.

Additions to the Library of Lectures will be made from time to time.

An up-to-date list of publications, films and film strips available is included in the Pony Club Year Book, published annually.

APPENDIX I

N.B. When the following lessons are being taught, instructors should refer to the paragraphs dealing with the subject, from both the rider's and the horse's angle, in "The Manual of Horsemanship", and other Pony Club Publications.

PLACING THE RIDER IN THE SADDLE

1. Read, "The General Purpose Seat" (Film Strip Book No. 7) and "The Manual of Horsemanship".

Place the Ride round the end of the manege.

2. Explain that a correct and independent seat is the foundation of all horsemanship; that we teach a General Purpose Seat which is readily adaptable for all forms of riding—should riders wish to specialise at a later stage.

3. Demonstrate and explain the General Purpose Seat: First settle in the centre and lowest part of the saddle, sitting up straight. This is most important. Then put the knee and thigh on the saddle and place the lower leg and foot. Fit the stirrups level with the sole of the foot. Take the stirrups.

Take up the reins; the hands should now be in contact with the horse's mouth and the legs with his sides.

Finally, hold the head up and the hips and shoulders square to the front, shoulders down.

4. Check each individual's position—ensuring stirrup-leathers are the correct length, and actually "placing" riders or correcting their faults where necessary. An Assistant Instructor or two can be useful here.

5. Explain and demonstrate very briefly the simplest aids to walk on, guide and to halt.

63

Turn the Ride into the track at the walk, correcting individuals' positions on the move.

6.   Demonstrate faults.

There are so many possible faults that it is better not to attempt to show them all at this stage. The Instructor should certainly demonstrate :

Too long a stirrup } with reasons (see Film Strip Book).
Too short a stirrup

He may show, if a rider is committing the fault :

Looking down.

Leaning forward and sitting on the fork.

Sitting on the back of the saddle or leaning too far back, with the feet forward.

Sitting crooked or with a stiff back.

7.   Demonstrate the correct seat once more.

8.   The Ride walks round again while the Instructor and assistants correct faults.

9.   Confirm the lesson by asking questions:

e.g., What happens if you ride with too short (or too long) a stirrup ?

Why should you not sit with your feet forward ?

Where should you look ?

A good Instructor does not try to make every rider conform to an exactly similar seat. If a rider has a good or moderate natural seat it is far wiser to help and possibly modify this natural seat, taking into consideration the rider's conformation and ability and the conformation and temperament of his horse. Much can be done by changing the rider on to another horse. For example, where a rider on a keen horse rides with a short rein and feet forward, a lazy horse will have the effect of bringing the feet and lower part of the legs back and enabling the rider to ride with a longer rein and lighter contact.

By watching a good demonstration and realising the reason for the application of the aids, etc., it is surprising how often a rider improves his own seat without being muddled by being told to keep his legs, hands, body, in a certain position.

An Instructor wants to avoid at all costs his Ride sitting tense and unnatural with reins in two hands and a fixed attitude. A relaxed, natural but alert seat is a joy to see—for example, a good horseman outside covert.

APPENDIX II

(A) TROTTING LESSON

1. Read "The Manual of Horsemanship". Have the Ride in a semicircle at the end of the manege.

2. Explain that the object of this lesson is to show how to ride at the trot.

3. Show how to make a horse trot—simple aids.

4. Explain the trot—a pace of two-time, the horse putting his feet down in pairs diagonally.

5. Demonstrate and explain two methods of sitting at the trot—sitting down in the saddle, or rising.
Elaborate: sitting down gives a firmer position and more control, but is tiring for long periods.
Demonstrate rising on alternate strides, showing the correct position, rising forward over the hands to allow for the forward movement of the horse.

6. Trot the Ride round behind an experienced leading file and get them rising.

7. Show the chief faults—too upright and too far forward. Show the right way once more.

8. Pick out individual bad cases and help them.

9. Rest after going around the manege a few times. Ask questions and then repeat.

10. Ask a few more questions to confirm the lesson, e.g.,
How does a horse put his feet down at the trot?
What ways are there of sitting at the trot ?
What is your chief fault ?

11. The instructor would not attempt to teach all the above in one lesson. He would concentrate on one aspect, rising perhaps, and later the simple aids for the trot.

12. In later lessons, when the correct rhythm and positions are established, the Class should be taught how to change diagonals and the reasons for so doing. This is an excellent preliminary exercise for pupils to learn to "feel" the paces of the horse before they are asked to name the leading leg at the canter.

(B) CANTERING LESSON

1. Read "The Manual of Horsemanship". Have the Ride in a semicircle at the end of the manege.

2. Explain that the object of this lesson is to show how to sit at the canter.

3. Demonstrate the canter—a pace of three-time.

4. Explain (cantering round again) that the horse leads with a fore-leg and hind-leg on the same side. On a circle a horse should lead with the inside leg.

5. Show how to make a horse canter—simple diagonal aids. Always start on a circle or corner to begin with.

6. Demonstrate the seat at the canter.

Sit down in the saddle with the seat bones moving slightly in rhythm with the horse and with the back supple.

7. Walk the Ride round the manege.

Ask, "What rein are you on?" "Which leg should you lead with?"

8. Make the Ride canter round behind an experienced leading file with plenty of room (at least one length) between horses.

They may, if required, be started "in succession".

Do not worry if they are on the wrong leg. Correct positions.

9.   Demonstrate the chief faults:
Seat bouncing on the saddle and stiff loins.
Leaning too far back and too stiffly; legs forward.
Leaning too far forward on the fork.
Demonstrate the correct seat once more.

10.   The Ride canters again and the Instructor corrects individual faults.

11.   Ask questions to confirm the lesson, e.g.,
What is the time or rhythm of the canter?
What are the simple aids to ask a horse to canter?
Describe the correct seat at the canter?
Check that each individual is clearly aware of his own faults and how to correct them.

(C) THE TURN ON THE FOREHAND

Position of the Class: down the side of the school, on the inner track, facing inwards.

1.   Tell the Class that you are going to teach them how to make their horses do a turn on the forehand.

2.   Demonstrate turns on the forehand to either hand.

3.   Explain the objects of the exercise.
   (a) By teaching the young horse to move away from one leg it is the first lesson in lateral movement.
   (b) It is an essential preparatory exercise for controlling the hindquarters.
   (c) It teaches the rider to use his legs independently, increases his knowledge of feel and the harmony of the aids in a simple preliminary to lateral work.

(d) Practically, it has many uses in everyday riding; especially when opening gates.

4. Demonstrate again a quarter turn, exactly as you will ask the Class to do it. Explain the correct aids.

5. The Class carries out the exercise in quick succession; each individual walking forward to the opposite track, coming to a square halt before making a quarter turn and immediately walking (or trotting) on round the track and back to his original place in the Ride.

6. Demonstrate the chief faults:

> Halt not still and square, with horse accepting the bit.
> Using too much rein; either the inner one too much with a resultant bend in the horse's neck, or both reins too much causing a backward movement.
> Not keeping contact with outer rein—horse walks forward.
> Lack of harmony of legs, seat and hands generally.

7. Demonstrate the correct movement again.

8. The Class carries out further turns and the Instructor corrects individual faults.

As the Class progresses they can be worked more actively on the move, turning across the school in two's, three's or even four's in open order.

Later, when ready for a half-turn of 180° the Class can be halted, a little in off the track in open order, and turned about, from the rear of the Ride, in quick succession, each member walking or trotting forwards 6-12 lengths before halting again.

9. Ask questions to confirm the lesson.

(D) SHOULDER IN

1. Read "The Manual of Horsemanship" and B.H.S. Booklet "Rules for Dressage".

Position of the Class—in a semicircle at short end of school.

2. Explain that the shoulder-in is a lateral movement where the horse is bent round the rider's inner leg. The outer shoulder is placed in front of the inside hindquarter. The inside legs pass and cross in front of the outside legs. The horse is slightly bent away from the direction of progress.

3. Demonstrate left and right shoulder-in, both on the track and down the centre-line, at a trot, stressing the fact that the forehand is brought in—and not the hindquarters pushed out.

4. Explain the aids—emphasising the necessity for working in an active collected trot, both before and during the exercise.

5. Demonstrate, as you will ask the Class to do the exercise, on a large half-circle across the school, asking only for a few steps of shoulder-in before riding *forward* again.

6. The Class carry out the exercise. Walk round the school, trotting in succession from the front of the ride to the rear, the Instructor correcting individuals.

7. Explain the objects:

    (a) It is one of the most important of all schooling movements.

    (b) By encouraging greater bending and engagement of the horse's hindquarters, it helps to lighten his forehand.

    (c) It supples the horse, particularly in his shoulders, joints and hindquarters.

    (d) It makes the horse more responsive and obedient to the aids, and improves his collection.

    (e) It improves the horse's stride and his physique.

(f) It improves the knowledge and harmony of the rider's aids.

(g) It develops the rider's sense of feel and of rhythm, and his knowledge of how to "position" his horse.

8. Demonstrate the main faults:

(a) Insufficient collection.

(b) Fading impulsion—losing the shoulder-in movement.

(c) Unlevel strides, especially if over-hurried.

(d) Incorrect rein-influence, i.e., hands too heavy and restrictive, inner rein too strong, causing bend in the horse's neck to be too great.

(e) Hindquarters escaping out rather than forehand brought inwards.

(f) Rider asking too much and too soon. The angle of the horse to the line of progress should bever be more than 45°.

(g) Tension; as soon as the horse's head is raised too high or he shows anxiety or even resistance, the rider must cease the exercise and must ride forward until calmness is restored.

9. Repeat the exercise on the other rein. The Instructor corrects individual faults and asks questions to confirm the lesson.

10. In subsequent lessons pupils should be taught to carry out shoulder-in down part of the long side of the school from or to a 10-15m. circle, and to use many variations of combination of shoulder-in to add to the variety of the horse's work. Remember to impress that they "must make haste slowly", never keeping the horse in shoulder-in for too long; always riding forward strongly afterwards.

(E) TURN ON THE HAUNCHES
OR DEMI-PIROUETTE AT THE WALK

N.B. The more advanced work covered in the later stages of this lesson should only be attempted with a Class of reasonably educated riders on schooled horses or ponies. For the correct sequence of preparatory work see Stages III and IV in the B.H.S. Publication "Training the Young Pony".

Position of the Class: In a semicircle, three lengths in off the track at one end of the school or manege.

1. Explain that whereas in the turn on the forehand the horse moves his hindquarters round his forehand, the reverse is the case in the turn on the haunches, or demi-pirouette, at the walk; for here the rider asks the horse to move his forehand with regular, clearly defined steps around his hind feet which mark time in walk rhythm on the spot as he turns.

2. Demonstrate a quarter turn of 90° to either hand, and then two about-turns (of 180°) on the haunches at the walk. Work in an active trot between the turns will facilitate maintenance of impulsion, and will shorten the demonstration time.

3. Explain the aids in detail, and confirm with questions that they all understand fully what they are going to try to do.

4. The Class carries out the 1st Exercise:

In two's, (later in three's) in open order. Quarter-turns across the school, the first turn, leaving the track, to be on the haunches. Each group repeats the exercise again before returning to its place in the Ride. Waiting members of the Ride should be asked to comment on the individual turns as each group finishes, to maintain interest and to improve their education.

5. Explain the uses of the Turn on the Haunches:

For the Horse.

(a) It teaches the horse further obedience to the rider's aids.

(b) As a physical training exercise it develops the muscles of the horse's back and hindquarters and improves the suppleness of his shoulders.

(c) It lightens his forehand and thus improves his balance and collection.

(d) It is a very good test of the correctness of his training, that he accepts the bit calmly, that he has sufficient impulsion and collection.

(e) It is an excellent preliminary to more advanced work, e.g.,pirouette in canter.

For the Rider.

(a) Practically it is a very useful turn, out hacking, or in the hunting field, being the smallest and most controlled turn.

(b) It improves the rider's knowledge and the harmony of his aids.

(c) It develops his feel, and thereby his efficiency and education as a horseman.

(d) By helping him to achieve a degree of collection combined with impulsion, it improves the rider's control of his horse.

6. After a short change of activity, such as some canter-work, the Class is lined up as before, and the 2nd Exercise is explained and carried out as follows:

Two members, one from each side of the Ride, e.g. Nos. 1 and 6 of a Ride of 10, trot forward and incline out to the track one on each long side of the manege, two lengths after B and E they walk, and on reaching the further quarter-markers in collected walk they about turn (180°) inwards, on the haunches. On completion of the turn they trot, pass right hand to right hand behind the Ride, two lengths after

E and B they walk, and repeat the turn on the haunches, this time to the opposite hand, trot, and return to their places in the Ride, for invited comments on their performances by Nos. 3 and 8, while Nos. 2 and 7 prepare to commence the exercise, and so on through the Ride.

7.   Explain and demonstrate to correct faults:

(a)   Any rough or exaggerated aid.

(b)   Insufficient preparatory collection.

(c)   Too much hand—horse shows resistance in his mouth; his head goes up; and in some cases the horse will step back, which is a very bad fault.

(d)   Impulsion not maintained sufficiently by rider's "forward aids" so that the horse loses the rhythm of the walk during the turn—one or both hindlegs give the impression of being "stuck" to the ground.

(e)   Rider's hips in opposition to the movement—or inner hip collapsed.

(f)   Rider looking down.

(g)   Rider's back stiff instead of supple.

(h)   Insufficient outside leg—horse's hindquarters swinging out.

(i)   Horse not correctly flexed, in the direction of the movement.

(j)   Insufficient outside, supporting, rein—horse wanders round, with too much bend in his neck.

8.   A 3rd Exercise consists of drilled Turns on the Haunches at the walk, by the whole Ride, working in open order, on two large (20m.) circles, one in each half of the manege, e.g. "On the large circle, in open order, Ride, on the Haunches, right-about TURN; and Trot . . ." and so on.

9.   When the Class has become proficient at the above exercises the canter strike off may be introduced immediately on completion of the Turn on the Haunches, e.g., left-about turn, and canter right; and vice versa. This is a very good exercise for the horse, and test for the rider. It is a particularly good exercise for achieving the correct canter from the walk.

Note.   Should difficulties arise for horse or rider, the Instructor must go back to easier work, i.e. turns of 90° or less, and must ensure that these are executed correctly and fluently before continuing with more ambitious work.

————————

APPENDIX III

(A) FIRST JUMPING LESSONS—POSITION

1. Read "The Manual of Horsemanship".

The lesson may be given in a manege or alongside a hedge. Two uprights and a pole are needed, and an assistant. Two oil drums to ride between will help to bring horses straight to the obstacle. A wing makes control easier.

The Ride is formed up facing the uprights.

Only quiet horses which will not rush or stop should be used.

2. Explain that the class is going to trot over the pole on the ground, which is quite simple.

3. Demonstrate trotting over the pole, hands on the mane, explaining the need to lean forward to keep in balance with the horse.

"Look forward; lean forward; hands on the mane".

4. The pole is removed but the uprights remain in position. The Ride carries out the exercise, trotting between the uprights ; when the horses are going quietly the Instructor puts the pole on the ground between the uprights and the Ride trots over it.

5. The Instructor forms up the Ride, raises the pole to about 1 ft. and trots over it. As his horse gives a little jump, he demonstrates and explains the correct position and how to maintain it.

6. The pole is put back on the ground and the Ride trot over it once more. While the Ride is still trotting round the Instructor gradually raises the pole until most of the horses make a little hop or jump. Stress the importance of holding on to the mane or neckstrap so as not to interfere with the horse's mouth, and of keeping in balance with the horse.

7. Demonstrate the chief faults:

Looking down and so causing a rounding of the back.

Losing balance and rhythm and thus being left behind or getting in front of the movement of the horse.

Jobbing the horse in the mouth.

Demonstrate the correct way again.

8. Repeat the exercise. The Instructor corrects faults.

9. Ask questions to confirm the lesson.

Note. If a child is riding a green pony the Instructor may run beside it and lead it.

(B) FURTHER JUMPING LESSONS—
USE OF THE REINS

1. Read the "Manual of Horsemanship".

An adjustable fence or cavalletti which can be raised for demonstrations and lowered for the Ride is required. Form up the Ride opposite and on the landing side of the fence.

2. Explain that up to date the Ride has only been learning how to sit on. Now, with reins, they will be in control of the horse throughout.

3. Explain further that a horse cannot put a foot to the ground in front of his nose. Therefore when landing he stretches out his head and neck.

The rider's hands must conform and maintain contact throughout the jump.

4.   Raise the fence high enough to make the horse jump.

Demonstrate the correct movement of the hands, following the movement of the horse's head and neck during the jump. The hands should keep the same light contact with the horse's mouth throughout. The bit, reins, hands and elbows should form a straight line. Watch and correct a tendency to push the hands up the neck or to bend the elbows excessively.

5.   Lower the fence. The Ride carry out the exercise.

6.   Demonstrate faults.

   (a) Emphasise the continual necessity for correct body position ; if the rider is out of time and 'left behind', the horse will get a job in the mouth.
      Result :—Either the rider is pulled out of the saddle or the horse's hind legs are pulled into the fence—or both !

   (b) Hands not giving horse sufficient rein. Results as above. Eventually the horse will refuse.

   (c) Hands forward too soon; lack of control. The horse can run out or jump crooked.

   (d) Leaving the hands out too long; lack of control especially when jumping a double.

It may be better not to show all these faults together but to wait until they occur.

7.   Demonstrate the correct way again.

8.   The Ride continue the exercise.

   Individual jumping and correction of faults.

9.   Ask questions to confirm the lesson, e.g.,Why is it necessary for the rider to keep contact with the horse's mouth ? What happens if the rider jobs the horse in the mouth ?

APPENDIX IV

WORKING A RIDER ON THE LUNGE

Purpose.

Lungeing, as an exercise, helps to develop in a rider the following qualities that one looks for in all good horsemen, whether they ride to hunt, ride to school or ride to jump:

1. Good balance.

2. A position from which it is easy to apply the aids as well as look attractive.

3. Independence of the hands and legs from the seat or body movements.

4. Development of feel to anticipate the movements of the horse.

The Instructor.

Before attempting to teach a pupil on the lunge an instructor must make certain that:

1. He has existing ability and experience in the correct technique of lungeing the horse. For further information in this respect refer to the Pony Club Publication "Training the Young Pony", pages 11, 12, 13 and 14. However, instead of a breaking pad, a normal saddle would be used with the adjustable side reins attached above the girth buckles.

2. He has the knowledge to correct the rider's position in the saddle as well as the ability to observe mistakes and correct them.

3. The horse is proved to go well on the lunge the very moments prior to putting a pupil up, especially should the rider be apprehensive or a beginner. It is at this stage that the horse's reaction to the whip and voice are assessed and the controlling aids established, so that the horse settles into even, rhythmical strides.

4. There is a suitable enclosed, for preference circular, space to lunge in.

5. The correct equipment, as listed below, is available.

6. He has gloves for lungeing and has taken off spurs should he have been wearing them for riding prior to lungeing.

Equipment.

It is essential that the correct equipment and saddlery is used and care has been taken to ensure a proper fitting, for without this there would be a possibility of lack of control of the horse resulting in a possible serious accident to the rider. A fall from the horse whilst being lunged is nearly always a serious one, for the centrifugal force of the horse travelling in a circle throws the rider outside the horse, possibly on to rails or boards surrounding the lunge ring.

The correct equipment consists of:

1. A lungeing cavesson, with a padded noseband and a jowl strap, properly fitted to stay in place so that the cheekpiece on the outside of the horse cannot hurt the eye or cause irritation.

2. A plain snaffle bridle with reins.

3. Adjustable side reins.

4. A 22 foot lungeing rein attached to the front D of the noseband.

5. A lungeing whip.

6. Brushing boots to protect the horses fetlock joints.

7. The Pony Club Saddle or an equally well-shaped saddle with a central-position seat.

Instructor's Assistant.

An able assistant to lunge the horse, enables the Instructor to take up a position from where he can see the rider from behind as well as from the side.

The Pupil.

The Instructor must carefully judge the ability of his pupil and adjust the duration and the variety of exercises to be performed in accordance with the rider's experience and fitness.

The exercises shown on the following pages should be taught the rider in the early stages with the support of the stirrup irons. However, as soon as progress can be made in the rider's confidence and balance, short periods without stirrup irons are preferable.

Should the rider lose position, the instructor must stop, show the rider how to correct himself and start again. As progress is made, the rider will recover lost balance and position in the same way whilst remaining on the move.

The easiest pace for the rider is a slow, smooth, rather idle trot, with the horse's head lowered rather than raised. Again, as the pupil progresses in his confidence, balance and coordination of movement, so the instructor can demand more activity and impulsion from the horse.

At all times be on the lookout for fatigue, for though a pupil's endeavour is to be encouraged, he will run the risk of muscle strain.

Finding Opportunities for Lungeing.

1. At a working rally with a small group of children at a time, each child taking a turn for a short period. These may be specially selected children from other classes who require concentrated and repetitive correction for riding faults.

2. At a working rally to encourage attendance of dismounted members.

3. To teach beginner riders so that they learn to fit their movements to those of the horse without being too concerned with the aids.

The Rider's Position.

Position at the halt.

Reference should be made to the "Manual of Horsemanship" in the opening chapter on "The Seat", and also to this handbook, pages 63-65.

The placing of the seat in the saddle has a direct influence on whether the rider is upright or crooked. The following exercise will assist the pupil to feel whether he is central and to enable himself to lay the thigh flat against the saddle.

Keeping the knee and ankle slightly bent, stretch the legs sideways from the horse's sides, hold them away for a shorter or longer period in accordance with the standard of the rider, then let them come back on to the saddle keeping the knee low.

Faulty positions to be watched for:

1. The seat slipping to the rear of the saddle, when it will be noticed that the rider's lower leg will be stretched forward and the upper part of the body leans too far back, or too far forward.

2. Leaning inwards, best seen from behind.

3. The rider's seat slipping across the saddle to the outside, when it will be noticed that the rider grips upwards with the inside knee and collapses in waist with possibly the inside shoulder lowered, and the head tilted to the inside.

4. The knee and thigh coming off the saddle unintentionally.

5. Turned out toes, when the correction would normally be to rotate the hip joint, so that the knees point to the front and this will naturally carry the toes towards the front.

6. The outside leg moving forward, due invariably to a collapse inwards of the hips and a leaning inwards and slightly backwards.

The correct position should be established at the halt and walk before commencing the trot.

Work at the trot.

This is the best pace for exercising the pupil once confidence has been established at the walk. In the beginning the pupil should hold on to the front of the saddle with both hands as lightly as possible, and they should play a part in pulling the seat to the centre of the saddle. As the pupil's confidence grows, simple individual arm exercises may be asked for; the pupil on the lunge will find it easier to retain balance when he holds the saddle with the outside hand. These exercises are of assistance in preventing the body from slipping and maintaining balance.

Work at the Canter.

Work at the canter is for advanced riders on the lunge, with horses that have acquired a well-balanced and shortened canter. It is tiring for the horse and the element of risk to the rider is greater due to the faster speed and greater centrifugal force, which may cause the seat of the rider to fly towards the outside of the saddle, whereupon the rider will in all probability grip with the calves.

Transitions of Pace.

Transitions of pace exercise the rider in maintaining balance and in following the movements of the horse's body during a moment of acceleration or deceleration, or through the change from one pace to another, and so develop independence of the hand and leg and strength in the upper body.

Work on Both Reins.

Needless to say, what is good for the horse is often good for the rider and no one in their right senses would consider lungeing the horse in one direction only.

The Exercises.

The Instructor must decide whether his pupil is "sloppy-supple" or "stiff" and choose exercises which will correct the faults. All exercises should be carried out, first at the halt, before doing them at the walk, trot or canter. As the pace increases so the exercises become more difficult to perform, particularly those requiring coordination.

Suppling, Muscling and Balancing exercises.

1. Individual arm circling, forwards, upwards and round.

2. Both arms circling.

3. Swing the lower leg forwards and backwards from the knee joint.

4. Position of the hands:

    (a) holding the saddle
    (b) down to sides
    (c) arms folded
    (d) held above the head, arms straight
    (e) hands behind neck keeping the elbows back
    (f) position for holding the reins.

5. Ankle circling.

6. Sitting with shoulders square and head turning slowly from left to right.

7. Arms swing forwards and backwards.

8. Arms to side and stretching sideways and above the head.

9. Arms stretching forwards, sideways, upwards and downwards.

10. Arms to side, and circling individually forwards, upwards and over at the same time twisting the trunk to touch the point of the horse's opposite hip.

11. Arms to side and a little to the rear; without body movement, bringing the heels alternately to touch the hand.

12. Similar exercise, though the hand will be thrust behind the back to touch the opposite heel without the body doubling forward.

13. Raising one arm, holding the saddle with the other hand and bending down to touch the other foot or the one on the same side.

14. Body bending forwards, upright and backwards.

15. Balancing exercise, arms stretched to the side, knee and thigh taken sideways off the saddle (short periods only).

Exercises at the Halt.

1. Round the world.
2. Clapping the heels above the croup.
3. Half scissors.
4. Scissors.
5. Pick up stick off the ground.
6. Back roll off.
7. Vaulting on (valuable for gymkhana events).

APPENDIX V

HORSEMASTERSHIP LESSONS (Dismounted)

1. Horsemastership is just as important as Horsemanship; the latter is described in an old Arab saying as "not the rider's performance but his consideration for his horse under all circumstances".

As much attention should be devoted to this subject as to riding. It has been found advantageous for a Branch to appoint some really experienced person as Horsemastership Adviser, whose job it is to find every means possible to improve members' general knowledge.

This may be done in a variety of ways, for example, by:

(a) Taking small groups or individuals at rallies.

(b) Taking small groups to visit well-run stables and explaining.

(c) Visiting neighbouring studs, veterinary surgeons, saddlers, farriers, dealers' yards, horse sales, racing stables, museums with horse relics, etc.

(d) Finding out and knowing anyone in the neighbourhood who can "talk the language" and asking them to talk to very small groups, either at rallies, or by taking groups to them.

(e) Shoeing inspection and advice at rallies.

(f) Bitting inspection and advice at rallies.

(g) Advice on unsafe, ill-fitting or worn saddlery at rallies.

(h) Being available at rallies to give advice on any individual pony problem for members and/or parents.

(i) Helping the D.C. (District Commissioner) in the super-
     vision of ponies at rallies.

(j) Arranging demonstrations and practice for stable
     management and routine, forage, first aid, clipping,
     trimming, mane and tail plaiting, shoeing, care of grass
     kept pony, etc.

(k) Being Master of Horse at camp.

2. To a large number of children Horsemastership is a dull
subject compared with riding though many, especially girls, find
great delight in looking after their ponies and even in cleaning
their tack.

To teach a subject which many may find dull is a considerable
test of the Instructor who will first have to create interest in his
class. This will depend largely upon the enthusiasm of the
instructor himself and upon the preparations made for the lesson.
Interest can be stimulated by the use of models and exhibits which
can be handled by members of the class. Such things as shoes
and shoeing tools, bones, diseased and healthy, of the legs and feet
(obtainable at any kennels), samples of forage, saddlery, bridles,
bits, etc., should always be available when the subject is to be taught
as well as diagrams of the foot and the skeleton, points of the horse
and such like.

Horsemanship can equally well be dealt with in summer or
winter, on a wet or fine day. Get under cover on a cold, wet
day and devote the Rally to this subject.

Avoid large classes. A crowd within a stable means that some
members see nothing and all have to wait too long for their turn
to practice the point under consideration. Riders should therefore
be divided into groups of five or six.

Avoid mixed classes of all ages. Teach by age groups or, better
still, by groups composed of members preparing for the same test.

Do not be too ambitious. Teach a little and teach it well.

Teaching by means of a game or a comic turn can make children "laugh and learn".

Aim at increasing general knowledge by giving five-minute talks and asking questions during rest periods in a Ride or whenever opportunity occurs.

3. Horsemastership may be taught by any of the "Various ways of Instructing" given on pages 3 to 5. Before deciding upon how to teach a subject an instructor must consider the various ways of doing so; this will largely depend upon circumstances and the means at his disposal such as the size, age and knowledge of the class, weather conditions, availability of accommodation indoors, projector, films, models, exhibits, etc. These points will be brought out in the lessons which follow.

But at some stage in these practical matters a lesson will have to be given.

(A) TEACHING GROOMING

First the Instructor must consider how he will teach the subject under the circumstances. If he has to deal with a large number of members on a wet morning at camp he may have no option but to show a film, provided the film, projector and room are available —as they should be. Or he may have a period allotted during camp or a rally when the subject is to be taught in the best possible way.

The day before he should look at the "Instructors' Handbook" and consider which of the "Various ways of Instructing" (pages 3 to 5) he will employ.

(i) The lesson. Dealing with an essentially practical subject like this, a lesson is absolutely necessary and it must be followed by practice. Here is a case of "What we have to do we can only learn by doing."

(ii) Demonstration. An essential part of a lesson. Arrange for somebody who really knows how to groom and has done so for a long time to give the demonstration.

(iii) Lecture. Too dull and too theoretical. The subject matter should be included in the explanations during the lesson.

(iv) Discussion. Question and Answer should be included in Confirmation at the end of the lesson.

(v) Film or film strip. Excellent but cannot take the place of Practice. After some practical instruction the film should certainly be shown. There are two films—"Grooming" and "Round the Stable Yard"—in the B.H.S. Film Library which deals with the subject.

(vi) Those working for a Test must certainly read "The Manual of Horsemanship". The best and most entertaining way of doing this is for a group to get together with the Instructor and for each member in turn to read out a paragraph. This can be combined with a demonstration.

Having thought the matter over the Instructor decides that a lesson, incorporating a demonstration by an experienced groom, is the best way to teach the subject; later a film on grooming will be shown; by this time the class should know enough to appreciate it.

The Instructor now sets about his preparations, the first of which will be to read over the section "Grooming" in "Horseman-ship". Next he decides that his Ride of twelve is too big to stand round one pony and so arranges with an assistant to take half; a competent groom will be warned to attend (he will have to do his demonstration twice, once to each half) and will be told exactly what he has to do; he may go through what he will do if there is any doubt. He will be asked to bring the items of the grooming kit illustrated in "The Manual of Horsemanship". Then arrangements must be made for two ponies to be available and two loose boxes, with straw, rugs or forms for the class to sit on. If fine, suitable places out of doors where the ponies can be tied up can be substituted for the boxes.

The Instructor should now be ready to give the lesson which should follow the normal sequence suggested on pages 5 to 13.

(a) Preparations. A small class of five or six are collected around the walls of a box in which a quiet pony is tied up with a head collar and rope. If out of doors a sheltered spot, out of the wind and, if very hot, out of the sun, should be chosen.

The grooming kit, including a miniature set if possible, should be laid out. The groom is ready to begin his demonstration.

(b) Explain the objects of grooming.

(c) Demonstration. The groom shows how the pony should be groomed. There are several good ways of setting about grooming but that given in "Horsemanship" should be followed, in view of the fact that tests are based on this book. The grooming should be accompanied by an explanation.

(d) Practice. On completion of the demonstration each member of the class will groom the pony in turn.

(e) Demonstration, accompanied by explanation, of the chief faults made by the class followed by the correct method once more.

(f) Repetition. The class repeats the grooming until all are doing it correctly.

(g) Confirmation by questions and practical tests that the Ride has mastered the lesson.

This lesson, a simple one but one which can easily become dull, has been explained in great detail in order to show exactly how any lesson should be prepared and taught.

Once more one must emphasise that the success of a lesson depends upon the trouble taken over preparations in ensuring that the Instructor knows his subject, has warned and briefed his assistants, has a place ready and has the necessary exhibits available. He must have an alternative in case of bad weather.

(B) TEACHING SHOEING

Every horseman should have some understanding of the care of a pony's feet and of shoeing.   "No foot—no horse" is an old and wise saying.

The teaching of shoeing to members of the Pony Club is on a different footing to, say, grooming, as the actual shoeing is a skilled job and must be done by a blacksmith, though it is very useful for a horseman to be able to remove a shoe in an emergency.

What members have to be taught, briefly, is the care of the pony's feet, to know when it needs re-shoeing and to recognise whether the shoeing has been correctly done.   In addition they must know the type and weight of shoe suitable to the work required of the pony.

Before starting to instruct, the Instructor will once more consider the "Various Ways of Instructing" (pages 3 to 5).

(i) The Lesson. As this is not a subject in which Practice must be taught, the lesson will not be used as such.

(ii) The Demonstration. This will be extremely valuable, in fact essential. The earliest demonstration should be in the blacksmith's shop, accompanied by a brief explanation. The class should not exceed five or six.

Another useful demonstration, after a visit to the blacksmith's shop, can be given by any Pony Club Instructor and always proves of great interest. It consists of showing the bones of a pony's leg and a hoof, a box of blacksmith's tools and nails in the proper box, a variety of shoes, and a section drawing of the hoof. Standing round a pony, sitting in a room or on the ground a full Ride of ten or twelve can be dealt with, the drawing being stuck up in front of the class and the items passed round from hand to hand.

(iii) The lecture.   A film-strip lecture is a suitable way of passing on the theoretical side of shoeing.   An excellent film strip lecture "The Foot and Shoeing" is available from Pony Club headquarters.   Large numbers can be instructed by this method at the same time.

(iv) Discussion, question and answers is of no value until the class has sufficient knowledge to give correct answers.   It may be used effectively after a demonstration or a film-strip lecture.

(v) The book "Manual of Horsemanship" deals very fully with this subject and should be known by all Pony Club members. The reading can well be fitted in with demonstrations or groups can sit round with members reading paragraphs in turn.

It will be seen that all the various ways of instructing, except the lesson, are suitable for teaching shoeing. It is better to start with practical demonstrations and then to pass on to the film-strip lecture.   Only a few spectators can be accommodated at one time in the blacksmith's shop and they must be dismounted;   this makes these visits difficult to arrange.   But small parties can go from camp or can be collected locally by an instructor when a member's pony is to be shod.   Below is an example of a demonstration:

VISIT TO THE BLACKSMITH'S SHOP

For members at Stage C2 in the Syllabus, Appendix X, page 123.

Preparations. Farrier's tools and shoes available and two ponies, one unshod with long unkempt feet and the other with thin, worn shoes, loose if possible, raised clenches, and with long feet. Room for five or six spectators; more will not be able to see.

The Instructor should read "The Manual of Horsemanship" and "The Foot and Shoeing".

Explanation and Demonstration.

Structure of the foot and names of different parts.

The need for shoeing; show the pony without shoes.

Difference between hot and cold shoeing.

Types of Shoes. Nails. Names of farrier's tools.

Show the pony to be shod. Explain indications that re-shoeing is necessary.

Blacksmith will now go through the six stages of shoeing, viz., removal, preparation, forging, fitting, nailing on and finishing.

What to look for in a newly shod foot.

Confirmation. By question and answer ensure that the class has mastered the lesson.

SHOEING DEMONSTRATION

For members at Stage C2 in the Syllabus, Appendix X.

Preparations.

Read "Horsemanship"—"The Foot and Shoeing".

Have ready a set of farriers tools in box, a selection of shoes and studs, a hoof with foot and leg bones, and a section diagram of the foot.

Arrange accommodation according to the weather; if outside or in stables a pony will be an asset. An instructor can probably deal with a class of a dozen.

Explain and demonstrate the need for shoeing, passing round the hoof and pointing to the pony's feet.

Assemble bones, giving names of most important, pointing out the laminae, "white line", the wall, pedal bone, navicular bone, pastern bones. Explain positions with the use of the diagram and the pony.

Show selection of shoes, fore and hind, fullered and plain, giving names of different parts, clips, calkins, feather-edge, etc., and their different uses.

Show and name farrier's tools, their names and uses.

Show the pony and explain indications that re-shoeing is necessary.

Explain difference between hot and cold shoeing.

Holding the correct tool explain the six stages of hot shoeing—removal, preparation, forging, fitting, nailing on and finishing.

What to look for in a newly-shod foot.

Confirmation. By question and answer ensure that the class has mastered the lesson.

If the members of the class have any knowledge of the subject much of the demonstration can be given by them coming forward and naming different parts of the foot, farrier's tools, shoes, etc. This will keep the class "alive" and they will enjoy displaying their knowledge.

(C) TACK CLEANING

Once again the Instructor asks himself how he will teach this subject thinking, as before, of the "Various Ways of Instructing" (pages 3 to 5).

This subject being one which members have to do they must certainly learn by doing it.   The lesson, including demonstration, will be the main instrument of instruction; after practical work, films may help.   A lecture is not so suitable; the subject matter is better included in explanations in the lesson and by means of question and answer.   It is also important that the book should be read.

This is perhaps one of the least exciting of the subjects to be taught; great trouble must therefore be taken in the collection and siting of exhibits, in having a really good demonstrator and an Instructor who makes lively and interesting comments as well as keeping the class on their toes by asking questions.

The lesson will follow the usual sequence.

Preparation. Read "The Manual of Horsemanship"–"Saddlery".

Collect a dirty, muddy saddle and bridle, cleaning materials as laid down in the book, saddle horse and a hook on which to hang the bridle.   The lesson may be given in a saddle room, where there is not much space, or outside where hooks will have to be improvised—perhaps on the branch of a tree or on a wall.   The best size for the class is five or six but double that number if outside.

Explain the necessity for well-kept saddlery for rider and pony and for the preservation of valuable tack.   Follow this with general remarks on the care of leather, lay out and explain the use of cleaning materials.

Demonstrate how to clean a saddle—strip, wash, soap and "put up".

Practice.   The class, perhaps working in pairs, will clean their own saddles.

The demonstrator will correct faults and show the correct way once more.

Finally the lesson will be confirmed by question and answers.

The same procedure will be followed in the cleaning of the bridle.

It is hoped that the above examples of lessons and of the manner in which an Instructor should set about preparing and giving them may not only help Instructors in teaching those particular subjects but may assist them in arranging the many other lessons in Horsemastership which must be taught if the standard of stable management is to keep pace with the high standard of riding in the Pony Club.

APPENDIX VI

PREPARING AND GIVING A TALK OR LECTURE

Preparing

Study. Knowledge of your subject will enable you to speak with confidence. Gain your knowledge from books and people and know your subject from different points of view should it be controversial.

Notes. Collect notes as a result of study.

Sequence. Arrange notes in sequence in which you wish to put them across.

Memory. If you have difficulty in remembering the sequence of your lesson, use a postcard, printing clearly the subject headings; but to lecture confidently you must have the detail in your mind.

Demonstration. The eye forms the window of the brain. Wherever possible, particularly with young people, demonstrate your subject.

Equipment and facilities. Decide what equipment and facilities you require for your demonstration and ensure that they are available and in good condition.

Assistance. Should you require assistance of another demonstrator be sure to brief him before the lesson, even though it may be a member of the class.

Timing. Know the time allotted for your lecture and plan to keep to this time.

Putting it across.

Confidence. Every good lecturer normally has apprehensive feelings before giving his lecture, though these disappear with his opening sentence if he knows his subject.

Salesmanship. You have knowledge to sell. Your class will not buy unless they have a good reason. The main reason should be value of the subject or lesson to the individual for his future use when working on his own.

Voice. You must be heard by all.

Starting. If you fear a shaky start, memorise your opening sentence. Whilst putting this across, you can be thinking of what to say to follow up.

Interest. Add variety to your voice by altering the pitch, the tone and the emphasis. Imagine your audience will not keep interested unless what you have to say compels their interest.

Mannerisms. Though these might help you they are often distracting to the audience. Look your class in the eye with confidence.

Questions. Ask questions and be questioned either during or, preferably, at the end of each lesson or lecture. This will give you the information on how much your class has learnt as well as drive the lesson home. MAKE THEIR MINDS WORK.

Continuity. Maintain continuity to what has already been learnt.

Sincerity. You MUST believe in what you say. If you lack sincerity it is hardly likely that your class will listen to you. This should be classed as perhaps the most important point in teaching.

Conclusion. Summarise your lesson and draw conclusions from your class. Know your closing sentence; if necessary memorise it.

Suggestions for Instructors. Read the "Instructors' Handbook" of the B.H.S., pages 1 to 13 and Appendix V, pages 89 and 92.

APPENDIX VII

THE WORKING RALLY

The "Working Rally" is the title adopted for Rallies where instruction is given. The ideal site must:

    (a) be easily accessible to members;

    (b) afford sufficient good and safe going for the number of members that may be expected;

    (c) if possible, afford some shelter from the elements if need arise;

    (d) if the Rally is to last all day, possess the necessary means to water and tie up ponies.

The sites, chosen in various parts of the Branch's area in order that all may have an opportunity of attending, may be selected by the District Commissioner (D.C.) or, the Branch Area Organiser, who may be more familiar with that particular part of the country.

Instructors will be invited to attend by the D.C. or the Chief Instructor appointed by the D.C. They should be warned beforehand what Ride they will be expected to take and the standard reached in the Syllabus of Instruction (see Appendix X), e.g., C 2 or B 1. Instructors should read in the Syllabus and in "The Manual of Horsemanship" what they will have to teach. It is convenient and ensures continuity if the same Instructors always take the same Rides.

All regular Branch Instructors should be provided, at the Branch's expense, with a copy of the following books:

"The Manual of Horsemanship"

"The Instructors' Handbook"

"Mounted Games and Gymkhanas".

At least three-quarters of an hour before the appointed time of the Rally, the person in charge should arrive, post notices, "To the Rally", and lay out the space available into maneges and a jumping ground. In general the more trouble taken in this matter the better. An almost bare field presents an unattractive picture but one in which ground plan flags are flying, notice boards erected, watering points indicated, chairs provided and a "splash" made suggests to the child mind that the Working Rally is an important occasion and the Pony Club a live organisation.

The Instructors should be on the ground half an hour before the rally in order to mark out their manege, where indicated, with flags, flower pots, sticks, stones or some such. They must inspect carefully and ensure that there are no rabbit holes, glass, etc., in their manege.

Instructors should be given an approximate timetable on which to base their day's work, which may well comprise Manege Work, Jumping, lunch interval and Games. A specimen of such a timetable will be found at the end of this Appendix, on pages 104 and 105.

They then go to their maneges and await their pupil's arrival.

Car parking needs attention to prevent cars becoming scattered all over the field. Parents should be invited to park cars in line in a place affording a good view of the whole proceedings.

The D.C., with perhaps one or two Associates as assistants, should wait near the entrance to the Rally field and, as members arrive, send them direct to their respective Instructors. If the members are not under control at once there may very likely be accidents from kicks, etc., as they bunch together and gossip. Rides should not exceed twelve members.

Members are usually divided into Rides according to the tests they have passed (and consequently the colours they are wearing), e.g., Blue Ride for A., Red Ride for B., etc.

Something should be arranged for dismounted members and newly joined members who have never been to a rally before, to ensure that they are introduced and made to feel welcome.

On arrival at their respective maneges, the members come under the control of their Instructor, who should ensure order and safety. The dumping of spare kit, clothes, etc., should be organised to ensure safety and prevent loss. Once the dumping is completed the Ride should walk round the manege and, when settled down, be formed up in the centre, and dismounted. An inspection of pony, saddlery and rider should then be carried out.* During the inspection one member should be detailed to write down the names of those attending. The efficient running of a Branch requires that names of members attending a rally shall always be recorded.

There are various methods of carrying out an inspection. One of these, is for members to inspect each other, in pairs.

The Instructor will then choose a Leading File, explain the programme and start work. Meanwhile the D.C., or somebody appointed for the job, should visit each Ride, collect the names and at the same time act as liaison between Rides in order to re-allot any member who may appear to be too advanced or too backward in any particular Ride.

A manege of 22 yards by 44 yards is a convenient size for a Ride of up to eight persons. For a Ride of more than eight the long side of the manege should be increased to 66 yards. The corners must be right angles. For very junior Rides, four corner markers may be all that is necessary, and it will be helpful to make the class ride outside the corner markers in order to prevent them cutting in. For the other Rides, quarter and half markers should be introduced and the class must ride inside the markers. It is suggested that 60 minutes is a sufficiently long period for Manege Work, the correcting of positions and teaching of the aids, etc.

*See notes on page 102.

Unfit Ponies or Saddlery.

With the steady growth of the Pony Club and the difficulty of finding sufficient ponies to mount its members, some instances of substandard conditions will inevitably be met with. This particularly applies in the case of many newly-joined members who are attending their first rally, for these have had no chance to understand the Pony Club's standards or traditions and, very often, have no family background of horse knowledge to guide them. It is the special duty and privilege of the Pony Club to play the part of counsellor and friend in such circumstances and this calls for sympathetic understanding and handling.

Strict adherence to the routine Inspection of rider, saddlery and pony at the start of every working rally (see page 101) is probably the best safeguard. Instructors should be alerted to dismount any member whose pony or saddlery is unfit or unsafe and to report the matter without delay to the District Commissioner or other Pony Club official who is deputed to be in charge of the rally. No other action by Instructors is advisable. If an approach to the parents concerned proves necessary or desirable, such should be initiated by the District Commissioner or the Branch Secretary.

Stable management.

A "Loose Box" made of baled straw is very convenient for giving a short lesson on stable management, while it forms, also, seats upon which the members can sit and hold their ponies behind them during a five-minute lecture.

Games.

Games form a very important part of the Working Rally. They create unconscious control of the pony and the children thoroughly enjoy them. Here again, safety must be a great consideration, and tact is necessary to ensure that games are chosen to suit the riders and ponies so that both and all can enjoy them. The book,

"Mounted Games and Gymkhanas", will be found helpful in selecting games to play. Be particularly careful to avoid dangerous ground and low overhanging boughs.

Games can quite well be organised by persons other than Instructors and can be taking place while others are receiving instruction.

Tests.

Tests are an excellent means of creating enthusiasm and ensuring progress. At every Rally examiners should be available to take tests for "D" and "C" Standards. Tests for "B" Standard are normally held once or twice a year and taken by examiners from outside the Branch (see the booklet, "The Pony Club Standards of Efficiency").

General Arrangements.

Rallies may be held in the morning, afternoon or evening, the main consideration being the convenience of members getting to and from the Rally. It is customary nowadays to commence at about 11 a.m., and finish at about 3 p.m. In this case members should bring halters with them and Instructors should supervise the watering and tying up of ponies during the lunch interval. Once the ponies are safely spaced and secured the members can then be free to mix and mingle as they will until the lunch interval is over.

At an afternoon Rally orange or lemon squash with some buns and cakes should be available before members start for home. Two or three dozen picnic mugs can usefully form part of the Branch "properties" (see Appendix VIII).

At least a quarter of an hour before the time to finish, the D.C. should sound a warning. Instructors can then make sure that their party finishes 'on a good note'. They should form their Ride up, look round the ponies and organise the collection of kit, etc. On a second warning sounded by the D.C., the members should ride past the D.C. and the host or hostess for the day and say "Thank You and Goodbye." The members will then disperse, but it is useful to have a small fatigue party to assist the D.C. in collecting the markers, jumps, etc., and in tidying up.

Every Pony Club rally should terminate by the members being assembled, officially "Dismissed" and sent home. This checks the tendency to hang about and to lark and do damage to the host's property. Further, what is equally important, should an accident occur after the official "Dismiss" has been given, the Pony Club cannot reasonably be held responsible.

A Working Rally on the above lines does work, so do try it. Branches who have persevered are now flourishing although when they first started they 'had not an Instructor in the countryside.' Make one person Chief Instructor and let others find their feet with Rides of six to eight members at the most. It will pay in the end far better than putting Rides of twenty or so under one person, however good that person may be. Rallies take place, for the most part, in the holidays and are attended voluntarily and for pleasure, so however diffident the young Instructors may feel, let them realise that they are giving their Ride enormous pleasure; let them be cheerful, happy and do their best and they can be assured that they are doing some good.

SPECIMEN TIME-TABLE FOR AN ALL-DAY PICNIC RALLY

The Westshire Hunt Branch of the Pony Club

Rally of Wednesday 12th August

ADMINISTRATIVE DETAIL

Place	Manor Farm, Downley.
Hour	11.00 a.m. to 3.00 p.m.
Organiser	The District Commissioner.
Committee Member in charge	Mrs. Jones.
Properties	Mr. Stone.
Hosts	Colonel and Mrs. Smith, Manor Farm.

PROGRAMME

11.00 a.m.	Rally	Mrs. Jones
11.15 a.m.	Equitation—Red Ride	Major Black
	Equitation—Green Ride	Miss Green
	Jumping—Yellow Ride...	Miss Brown
	Grooming—Dismounted members ...	Mr. Brick
12.00 noon	Lecture—Red Ride	Major Black
	Jumping—Green Ride	Miss Green
	Equitation—Yellow Ride	Miss Brown

12.30 p.m.   Water, off saddle and tie up to Lines
under Ride Instructors in the order
Yellow Ride, then Green Ride, then
Red Ride.

1.00 p.m.   Picnic Lunch

1.30 p.m.   Rally dismounted. Talk: "Our Puppy
Show next week" by Colonel Read,
M.F.H.

2.15 p.m.	Saddle up	
	Jumping—Red Ride	Major Black
	Games—Green Ride	Miss Green
	Games—Yellow Ride	Miss Brown
3.00 p.m.	Rally	Mrs. Jones
	Notices	Branch Secretary
	Thanks to Hosts	Mrs. Jones
	Dismiss.	

NOTE : Will Mr. Stone and all Ride Instructors please meet Mrs. Jones
on the ground not later than 10.15 a.m. to set up the jumping
lane and mark out the maneges.

Copies to : All Members of Committee
All Ride Instructors.

APPENDIX VIII

PROPERTIES FOR A WORKING RALLY

Properties are a great asset to a Branch. They eliminate improvisation, begging and borrowing and are labour saving.

The purchase of items of equipment is, however, a drain on Branch funds and can only be dealt with as a long-term policy spread over several years. Although in some cases the initial cost may be high, the expense should be nonrecurring provided the equipment is properly cared for.

It is a good idea to appoint one member of committee to accept responsibility for the storage and maintenance of properties and their provision on the ground as and when required.

There are two essentials for Pony Club properties. Firstly they must be compact and secondly, light in weight. The guiding principal should be that all the properties required for a Working Rally can be loaded into and transported in a shooting brake or estate van.

The following have proved useful at Working Rallies :

1. **Direction Boards.** "To the Rally"—obtainable from Pony Club Headquarters.

2. **Attendance Book.** For recording names of members present and other things, such as sale of badges, orders for ties, etc.

3. **Manege Markers,** such as ground pegs (broom handles sawn in half and pointed at one end) and flags; tins painted and lettered; land drainage pipes; electric fencing posts and binder twine, etc.

4. **Portable Jumps.** These offer opportunity for display of ingenuity in their construction. On the whole, however, "Cavalletti" are the best initial investment on account of their adaptability to various heights and types of jump. (See "Manual of Horsemanship"–"The Use of Cavalletti").

5. **Equipment for Horsemastership Instruction.** This includes a set of grooming kit, shoeing tools and shoes, bones of the horse's foot and foreleg, samples of forage, bits and articles of saddlery and of clothing.

6. **Equipment for Games.** Five pails and twenty old polo balls supply all the equipment necessary for at least five different games. Other useful items are china eggs and Woolworth dessert spoons, polo sticks and rubber balls, sacks, bamboo sticks, a 'cushion' for Cushion Polo, coloured arm bands for team games, boards, foolscap paper, paper clips and pencils for written competitions, and a copy of the book "Mounted Games and Gymkhanas".

7. **Notice Board** and drawing pins for the display of notices, viz. a copy of the current fixture list, the programme for the day, schedules of forthcoming shows in the district, memory joggers such as "Have you paid your subscription?", particulars of ponies wanted or for sale, articles of outgrown riding clothes for sale or exchange, Pony Club publications and the results of Inter-Branch competitions.

8. **Whistle Sticks** for instructors and for umpires during games. Made by the local saddler and similar to those used by umpires at polo.

9. **Ropes for Horse Lines.** These should not exceed 90 ft. or they may be too heavy to carry. They may be secured to a row of trees or run out in a straight line with picketing posts. In either case it is advisable to anchor one end around a tree trunk for greater safety.

10. **Water Buckets** for watering ponies. Those provided under 'Equipment for Games' (see para. 6) serve both purposes.

11. **Litter Receptacles.** Sacks answer well, particularly if marked as Litter receptacles and hung in prominent places. At the end of the Rally they can be tied at the neck and deposited in the trunk of a car for emptying at home.

12. **Car Parking Notices,** such as "Please Park Cars Here" and "Horse Boxes Park Here".

13. **Chairs** for the use of the committee and spectators.

14. **Mugs and Drinking Straws** for drinks.

15. **Flagpole,** tubular, aluminium with flag in Pony Club colours. (See list of P.C. Supplies in Year Book.)

16. **Branch First Aid Box.**

A USEFUL TYPE OF LITTER RECEPTACLE

APPENDIX IX

HUNTING AND COUNTRY LORE

The Pony Club Organisation Committee has produced a pamphlet on this subject which includes a series of tests which may be taken by members who have attained "C" and "B" Standards in equitation.

The success of the idea depends entirely upon choosing the right Instructors, who must:

(a) Really know the subject and not just quote from books;

(b) Be genuine lovers of the countryside;

(c) Be enthusiastic to put over the subject to children, and have the ability to talk to them as companions rather than as pupils.

Branches should appoint "Hunting and Country Lore Instructors" whose task is to take "Rides" for hacks.

1. These hacks vary in length (e.g. a picnic hack or a twenty-minute-or-so hack) to fit in the Working Rally programme.

2. These Instructors need know no more about teaching riding than is necessary to teach hunting or hacking etiquette, such as how to negotiate a gap or gate, and how to behave when riding across another person's property.

3. Instructors should reconnoitre suitable rides in the required area so that when the time comes all the hundred-and-one things of interest that can be shown to children during a country hack are readily brought forth.

4. A broad summary of the subject matter would be:

Estate Management: landlord and tenant; maintenance of agricultural land, forests, fences, paths, woodland rides, water and services.

Farming: Stock and crops and their recognition; buildings, implements, fences, gates; damage due to hunting and its prevention.

Natural History: Animals, birds, trees, copse wood, flowers, seasons.

Hunting:

(a) Etiquette.

(b) Description of actual hunts that have taken place in that country.

(c) Imaginary situations that might occur; Hounds, Hunt Servants, M.F.H. (Master of the Fox Hunt), the Field.

Language and Customs: Hunting expressions, Hound language, local expressions and customs.

Shooting and Fishing: Preservation and rearing, seasons, sporting rights.

There is so much of interest that those born and bred on a farm or large estate have learnt almost unconsciously but which those without that opportunity cannot have learnt. Without knowing these things or being able to understand the situation from the Landowner's and Tenant's point of view, it is impossible to appreciate fully the joys of Hunting or to play one's full part in supporting the local Hunt.

HUNTING AND COUNTRY LORE TESTS

INTRODUCTION

There shall be three standards. Stages I and II to be awarded only to those who have attained 'C' standard in Equitation and Stable-Management. Stage III to be awarded only to those who have attained 'B' Standard in Equitation and Stable-Management. Otherwise these Certificates are awarded independently of the Equitation and Stable-Management tests.

The object of these tests is firstly to encourage Branches to teach and members to learn subjects which will greatly enhance the enjoyment of riding in the country, and finally to award a Stage III certificate which shall not be merely a conciliatory gift for the person who is unable to attain an 'A' for Equitation and Stable-Management, but shall be a meritorious award to those, who, by good endeavour, have learnt to be good citizens of the countryside and good foxhunters.

NOTES FOR INSTRUCTORS AND EXAMINERS

1. These Tests are essentially practical (see "Instructors' Handbook" Appendix IX). The Pony Club publications, "Riding to Hounds" and "Five-Minute Lectures — Foxhunting", will serve as books for reference for Foxhunting. The Young Farmers' Club can help with lectures and their publications "Forestry" and "The Farm" will help Stage III candidates.

2. The Examiner, who will need to have adequate knowledge of the locality, shall be appointed by the District Commissioner. Candidates may only take the test by permission of the District Commissioner of the Branch to which they belong.

3. In each Stage the District Commissioner will advise the Examiner that candidates have attained the required standard in Equitation and Stable-Management, and for Stage III will satisfy the Examiner that the required approval of the local Hunt has been attained. The Examiner should ensure that candidates can attire themselves correctly for the Hunting Field according to their age.

4. **NOTES REFERRING TO STAGE I.**

Part 2　Country Lore

(*a*) These candidates are of an age when they ride unaccompanied by an adult. For the sake of their own safety and the safety of other users of the road, they must have a common sense knowledge of the Rules applicable to riding on the public roads.

(*b*) This should not be a "Law Examination", but candidates should prove that they have an awareness of where they may ride and where they may not ride.

(*c*) A knowledge of afforestation is not necessary, but the candidate should appreciate that damage and annoyance to woodland owners is caused by ponies treading on or nibbling young trees, by unnecessary treading in of ditches, by treading down of wire or leaving gates open, as well as by the disturbance of game.

(*d*) Knowledge of agriculture need be very slight. However, candidates should show that they notice such simple things as fields that have been ploughed, drilled, rolled or harrowed, fields holding flocks or herds, and the difference between new grass and old, standing crops and root crops.

Part 3. Foxhunting

Everything should be done to encourage candidates to learn from instruction and practical experience. Conditions vary so much in various hunting countries, also the relationships between Hunt Officials and children, that one can only advise the Examiner to use the Test Card as a guide and the examination as an encouragement

5. NOTES REFERRING TO STAGE II.

Part 2. Country Lore and Agriculture

(a) and (b). It is recommended that this is a practical test carried out during a ride or drive around the countryside. The candidates should satisfy the examiner that they really do take an interest in what goes on around them in the countryside. At this stage a keenness and an obvious wish to learn with a slight knowledge is as important as anything.

Part 3. Hunting

(a) and (b). At this stage the candidates should prove that their hunting education has progressed beyond merely riding and that an awareness of the chief characteristics of the hound and the quarry is dawning.

(c) The candidate should realise that a Hunt entails much management and does not just happen. One day he or she must help. Hunting should be fun but its administration must be taken seriously.

(d) The candidate should show enough understanding to satisfy the examiner that the interest is there. Refer to Pony Club publication "Riding to Hounds".

(e) Candidates should realise that the Hunt Servants are servants and "in the field" have a job to do. The Huntsman hunts the hounds; the whipper-in serves the Huntsman.

(f) Hunting is so much more fun if candidates can know what is happening, by recognising the more frequently used sounds. They will be less afraid of standing or riding on their own if they know they will not be left nor be in the way.

6. NOTES REFERRING TO STAGE III.

Part 2. Country Lore

It is not suggested that candidates should have studied 'Law'. They should, however, realise the rights of equestrians as ratepayers to have their interests looked after by the appropriate Council. They should have learnt how to approach a local Council and their right to do so.

(a) *Woodlands* Book of reference from library of Young Farmers' Club, "Forestry".

(b) *Agriculture* The local Branch of the Young Farmers' Club will surely co-operate in supplying lecturers. Ref. Y.F.C. publication "The Farm".

An elementary knowledge of these two subjects is essential if one is to understand and get to know one's neighbours who live on the land; to appreciate their point of view, and to share to some extent their lives. Unless we can do this, we will remain to the countrymen strangers who are unwelcome to ride their land, and, therefore, unwelcomed followers of the Hunt.

Part 3. Hunting

Much of this will need discussion between the M.F.H. (or his appointed) and the District Commissioner (or his appointed). It is appreciated that candidates should not be expected to "Visit" on behalf of the hunt unless carrying messages from Hunt Officials.

HUNTING & COUNTRY LORE TEST — STAGE I

Candidates must have passed P.C. Tests for 'D' & 'C' standard in Equitation and Stable-Management.

Part 1. STABLE-MANAGEMENT:

(a) Care of pony before and after Hunting

(b) Condition of pony and examination of shoes

(c) Turn-out of pony

(d) Care, inspection, and fitting of saddlery

(e) Riders turn out. Correct wearing of clothes and carrying of Hunting Whip.

Part 2. COUNTRY LORE:

(a) Know Pamphlet "Riding & Road Sense" (P.C. publication). Also, be sure to find out and learn local variations of road signals and rules.

(b) Appreciate the significance of the designations: Public Right of Way for Vehicles, Bridle Road, Footpath, Private Road, Permitted Rights of Way.

(c) **Woodlands :** Recognise 3 Hard Wood and 2 Soft Wood trees most common in vicinity.

Recognise plantations, whether wired or unwired, and areas cleared in order to encourage self-regeneration.

Elementary understanding of game preservation. Breeding seasons. Rearing Fields.

(d) **Agriculture:** Recognise: Old pastures, new grass and drilled fields. Wheat, Oats, Barley when in ear. Kale and Root crops. Cows, Heifers, Bullocks. Lambing pens, sheep grazing in flocks. Brood Mares and young stock.

Part 3. HUNTING:

1. Name M.F.H., Secretary and Hunt Servants (Christian name allowed) who appear in the "Field". Address of Secretary and Kennels.

2. Realise the M.F.H.'s authority and normal procedure of riding to hounds when at Meet, at the Covert side and when hounds are hunting or cub-hunting.

3. Open and shut gate or put up or take down rails or wire mounted and dismounted.

4. Purpose of Cub-hunting as opposed to Regular Hunting and time of year each takes place.

5. Know more commonly used Hunting expressions which might cause embarrassment if not known, e.g., Hunt Servants, The Field, The Meet, Drawing a Covert, Hounds Running, Checked, Hit Off Line, Throwing Their Tongues, Couples, etc. Selected from "Five Minute Lectures—Foxhunting", lecture 13.

6. Positioning of pony (a) when hounds or hunt officials pass (b) when asked to hold up, view a fox and when a fox is viewed and hounds are being brought up to the holloa.

7. Use of Hunting Whip as a warning to hounds and for opening and shutting gates.

HUNTING & COUNTRY LORE TEST — STAGE II.

Candidates must have passed P.C. Tests for 'D' & 'C' Standard in Equitation and Stable-Management.

Part 1. Recap on all subjects as laid down for the Stage I Hunting Certificate.

The candidates to prove that since gaining Stage I they have become more confident in that knowledge.

In Addition

Part 2. COUNTRY LORE

(a) **Woodlands:** Should prove that they have observed undergrowth in Woodlands, Privet, Briar, Bracken, Heath, Gorse (Whin), Rhododendrons, Hazel, Blackthorn.

Conditions likely in coverts under certain trees. Bare under mature timber, thick plantations, copse cutting, marsh and willow.

Be able to name some coverts in own vicinity, the owner, and describe roughly their conformation and whereabouts.

(b) **Agriculture :** Describe the route of a 2-hour hack around their home, naming the occupiers of farms or coverts, the bridle ways, etc., the hedgerow growth and fences, animals and birds that they can recognise. Show a reasonable idea of how a neighbouring farmer makes a living, i.e., dairy, sheep, etc.

Part 3. HUNTING

(a) **The Fox:** correct terms when speaking of. Its natural way of life.

(b) **Foxhound:** Correct terms when speaking of. Whelps, Young Hounds & Walks. Entry. Feeding and conditioning. Kennel accommodation.

(c) Management of Country: Show an interest in Committee, Subscribers, Farmers, Supporters' Club, Landowners, Subscriptions, Xmas Boxes, raising funds by Pt.-to-Pt. (point-to-point) etc., Earth Stoppers, Keepers.

(d) "In the Field": An interest and understanding of hunting by scent.

Effects of ground surfaces and wind upon scent. Distraction caused to pack by holloaing and horses moved during a check.

A sensible recognition of Huntsman's task.

A sensible recognition of Whipper-in's task.

(e) Recognise by sound if Huntsman is drawing a covert, blowing hounds away, collecting hounds, blowing out of covert, casting his hounds, has accounted for the fox.

Part 4. MAP READING:

Have a rudimentary knowledge of 1 inch Ordnance Survey map and be able to plot and follow a route on it.

HUNTING & COUNTRY LORE TEST — STAGE III

Candidates must have passed P.C. tests for 'D', 'C' & 'B' standard in equitation and Stable-Management.

Part 1. RECAP ON STAGE II TEST:

In order to gain a Stage III Certificate the Candidate should be known to the M.F.H., Secretary or Huntsman, or all three, as a person who can be trusted and who does help "In the Field" and at home.

Part 2. COUNTRY LORE:

An elementary knowledge of Local Government, Parish Council, Rural Council, County Council, Local Authority's responsibility to provide safe surfaces for horses on Highways. Local Authority Map of Bridle Ways, and who to approach if Bridle Roads are blocked, overgrown, etc.

(a) **Woodlands:** Elementary knowledge of forestry and care of Coverts, including Ride Trimming.

Recognise the Hunt's obligation to covert owners.

Recognise Trade (i.e., indication that a covert, etc., is used) by Foxes, Badgers, Rabbits, etc.

(b) **Agriculture:** Recognise importance of farming as an industry, and a reasonable overall appreciation of the means of production of crops, stock.

Recognise the Hunt's obligation to farmers.

Be on friendly terms with and therefore well known to several farming families in the country.

Part 3. HUNTING:

Pay an annual subscription (monetary or in kind) to the Hunt.
A knowledge of the care of puppies at Walk.
Know how to "Put an earth to".
Has seen and can recognise an "Earth" used by cubs.
Understands procedure in reporting damage and making good if necessary.

Can assist the Hunt Officials by obtaining local information if required to do so, i.e., by Visiting Farmers, Earth Stoppers, Covert owners, etc.

Can confidentially be used by M.F.H., "In the Field" to help during the day's hunting, watch a ride, or side of covert, hold or lead a horse, fetch a terrier, take a message, assist a whipper-in or the hunt secretary.

Takes an interest in hounds, and is able to talk sensibly about the hunting qualities of hounds "In the Field".

From practical experience can converse on all that is written in "Riding to Hounds" and "Five-Minute Lectures — Foxhunting".

APPENDIX X

A SYLLABUS OF INSTRUCTION

FOR THE PONY CLUB

This syllabus has been produced to assist Instructors to cover all the ground necessary for the various standards and so that they may know, on being called upon to take a Ride at any stage, what to teach.

The whole course has been divided into stages, each of which corresponds to a year's instruction. At the end of certain stages tests will be taken by those who are considered up to the standard.

Some members will, of course, progress faster than others, and will ride better. Whilst these should not be held back, it is important that they should follow the sequence and not miss any part of the syllabus. Care must be taken, in promoting members to a higher stage, that they are up to the standard in riding and in knowledge; a practical test will be necessary.

The training of every pony is capable of improvement. The syllabus therefore contains suggestions for movements, which should be within the capacity of riders at the relevant stages of the training of the pony. It is not intended that eleven years should be spent in training a pony, but members will change their ponies once or twice at least during this time and reference to the syllabus will indicate movements suited to the pony and to the ability of the trainer. Those who can ride should follow the sequence in training a young pony which might be expected to reach stage A in about two years' continuous training.

Even to attempt to improve the training of a pony is an admirable way for a rider to improve his riding, making him less self-conscious and introspective and increasing his confidence.

The items shown under "Other Instruction" include the essential practical and theoretical knowledge, without which it is impossible to become a good horsemaster or to pass the Pony Club standards.　In the syllabus these matters should be dealt with fully and exhaustively at the proper time, so as to ensure a solid foundation of knowledge which will not be forgotten.　If this is done, the average member should pass the tests in these subjects without difficulty.

It is necessary to stress the importance of continuous repetition and revision.

SYLLABUS FOR THE PONY CLUB

(Stages correspond approximately to a year's instruction)

Stages 1 and 2. Elementary.

Take test for Standard 'D' at about the age of 8 or 9.

Stages D1, D2, D3.

The attainment of a firm seat and the application of simple aids.

Take test for Standard 'C' at about the age of 11 or 12.

Stages C1, C2, C3.

Training as an active horseman who knows the reasons for what he is doing, and can ride over fences at all paces.

Take test for Standard 'B' at the age of 14 or over.

Stages B1 and B2.

Improving as an active and effective horseman able to apply the aids efficiently, capable of riding an unknown horse, and able to teach a horse the aids.

Take test for Standard 'A' at the age of 16 or over.

Stage A. For those who have passed Standard 'A'.

Training to improve horsemanship and widen experience. Should aim at becoming an instructor and an expert trainer of a young horse.

STAGES 1 & 2—ELEMENTARY

RIDING

Mounting and Dismounting.

How to hold the reins.

Place in saddle and correct seat.

Ride without a leading rein.

Game.—"Follow my leader".

OTHER INSTRUCTION

How to approach and handle a pony.

Catch pony and put on head collar.

Lead a pony in hand.

Proper way to give a pony an apple or carrot.

Name simple points of the pony.

Name saddlery.

Take Test for Standard 'D' at age of 8 or 9.

TRAINING OF PONY

Pony to stand for mounting.

Pony to lead and answer to voice.

STAGE D1

RIDING

The next objective is the attainment of a firm seat independent of the reins, and the application of elementary aids.

Turnout.

Mounting and dismounting.

Correct position in the saddle.

Hold reins correctly.

Balance exercises at halt.

Walk without stirrups.

Position at the trot.

Increase of pace and use of the legs.

Decrease of pace.

Independent work in the open.

Hunting. Can, if wished, be blooded as soon as able to ride to the meet and after the hounds.

Games: Flag picking, Musical Mugs, Grand Chain.

OTHER INSTRUCTION

The Highway Code and correct signals.

The Points of the Horse, Colours, Markings.

Care and working of a pony off grass.

Saddling and bridling.

Picking up feet.

Lead horse in hand at walk and trot and turn about

Hunting: Preparation of rider and pony for hunting. Training and condition of pony.

Turnout of horse and rider.

How to take a horse in and out of a trailer or horse box.

TRAINING OF PONY

The first objects to be attained are confidence and obedience, free forward movement and response to the rider's leg.

Stand to mount and dismount.

Stand still and quietly.

Answer legs and move forward at walk and trot.

Walk away from other ponies.

STAGE D2

RIDING

Repeat Stage D1.

Balance exercises at walk.

Short trot without stirrups.

Tighten girth when mounted.

Increase and decrease of pace.

Use of hands (open rein) in simple turns and circles at walk and trot.

Position at canter.

Walk on loose rein.

Ride up and down hill.

Independent work.

Trot over heavy (e.g. telegraph) pole as preliminary to jumping.

Games, Bending race. Visiting.

OTHER INSTRUCTION

Names and uses of essential grooming kit.

Elementary care and cleaning of saddlery.

Picking out feet.

Treatment of minor wounds.

Recognise lameness.

Know main indications of health in a horse.

Hunting, Organisation of the Local Hunt.

The country. Kennels. History.

Master and Hunt Staff. Names and duties.

Committee. Subscribers. Farmers.

Finance.

TRAINING OF PONY

Repetition of Stage D1.

Move forward freely at walk and trot.

Simple turns and circles (open rein) at walk.

Increase and decrease of pace.

Canter.

Work up and down hill.

Independent work away from others.

Lead in hand over low poles and small ditches or send round loose school if available.

STAGE D3

RIDING

Repeat Stage D2.

Trot without stirrups.

Alter stirrups when mounted.

Free walk.

Walk or trot on loose rein.

Canter on named leg on circle.

Independent work.

Jump cavalletti, very small fences and tree trunks.

Repetition before Test C.

Games: Handkerchief snatching. Touch Wood.

OTHER INSTRUCTION

Elementary feeding, watering and cleanliness of the pony.

Recognise a loose or worn shoe, risen clench, excessively long foot and know what action to take.

Know when a horse needs shoeing and what to look for in a newly-shod foot.

Measuring and height of a pony.

Hunting : Attacks on hunting. British Field Sports Society. Organisation of the country.

Coverts. Stopping.

Revision.

Revision of Highway Code.

Take Test for Standard 'C' at age of 11 or 12.

TRAINING OF PONY

Repetition of Stages D1 and D2.

Walk and trot on loose rein.

Walk and trot over ridge and furrow.

Simple turns and circles (open rein) at trot.

Canter on circle on named leg.

Walk and trot over heavy (e.g. telegraph) pole as preliminary to jumping.

Trot over cavalletti and small fences.

Good manners should be insisted upon—e.g. quiet with other ponies, traffic, dogs, hunting whip, polo stick, etc. Must stand when required.

STAGE C1

The objective now is to produce an active horseman who knows the reasons for what he is doing and can ride over fences at all paces.

RIDING

Turnout, Mount and dismount on either side.

Position at walk, trot and canter.

Stirrups still fairly short.

Balance exercises at trot.   Trot without stirrups.

Alter stirrup and girths when mounted.

Increase and decrease of pace.

Stronger trot and slow trot (sitting).

Turns and circles (direct rein) at trot.

Time and rhythm.   Study of action and paces.

Trot on either diagonal.

Canter on circle on named leg.

Work on loose rein at walk, trot and canter.

Quarter turn on forehand.

Halt and salute.

Elementary Riding School Drill. Jump low poles and tree trunks with reins and stirrups at trot and canter.

Ride over small ditches with reins and stirrups at trot and canter.

Independent work.

Open gate with hand.

Ride up and down steep hills and banks.

How to show a pony.

Games: Mock Hunt, Ball and Basket and other simple gymkhana competitions.

Cushion polo.

OTHER INSTRUCTION

Good and bad points of conformation.

Understand care and working of pony off grass and of a corn-fed, stabled pony.

Know articles of grooming kit and be able to use them.

Fit saddlery.

Care and cleaning of saddlery.

Loading and unloading a horse in trailer or horse-box.

Care of pony on return from hunting.

Hunting: The Fox.

The Foxhound.

Breeding, Walking, Feeding, condition and exercise.   Entering and cub-hunting.

Revision.

TRAINING OF PONY

The object in the next stage is to make the pony supple, teach him to balance himself, and to respond to the aids. He should accept contact with the bit. He should jump small fences kindly in cold blood.

Repeat Stages D1, D2, D3.

Stronger and ordinary trot.

Turns and circles (direct rein) at trot.

Work on loose rein at walk, trot and canter.

Quarter turn on forehand.

Jump cavalletti, tree trunks and small ditches at walk, trot and canter.

Stand to open gates.

Work up and down steep hills and banks.

Balance.

Hunting: Take pony out for short days cub-hunting or hunting.

Ride about quietly.

Don't overface at fences.

Elementary Hunter Trials.

STAGE C2

RIDING

Repeat Stage C1.

Mount without stirrups.

Work hard at strengthening seat.

Some lengthening of stirrups on the flat.

Stronger use of legs in rhythm.

Independence of hand and leg.

Use of hand and leg in harmony.

About turn on forehand.

Bits and their uses.

Double bridle. How to hold reins.

Ordinary and stronger canter.

How to show a pony in the ring.

Jump various small fences and ditches at trot and canter with and without reins and stirrups.

Deal with refusals. Use of stick.

Independent work.

Open gate with hand and whip.

Walking through ford.

Ride up and down steep hills and through thick and 'blind' places.

Gallop.

Games: Musical poles. Egg and Spoon race. Other gymkhana competitions. Cushion polo. Polo stick and ball.

OTHER INSTRUCTION

Know principles of watering and feeding, and be able to put these into practice.

Some knowledge of the different items of forage.

Know the principles of exercising and how to get a horse fit.

Rug up and bandage.

Shoeing.

Names and uses of farrier's tools.
Names of different parts of the foot.
Names of different parts of the shoe.
Different types of shoes.
Points in good shoeing.
'Roughing', frost nails, Screw cogs. Mordax Studs.

Biting.

Teeth and Ageing.

Hunting by scent. Cub-hunting. Cubs. Young Entry. The Field. Hunting the Fox. Drawing. Finding. The Check. Casting hounds. The tired fox. Killing foxes. Digging.

Know how to prepare a horse for travel and feed on a journey.

TRAINING OF PONY

Repeat Stages D1, D2, D3 and C1.

Double bridle or pelham may be introduced.

About turn on forehand.

Stronger canter.

Jump larger fences and ditches with greater variety.

Walk through ford and thick and blind places.

Steady gallop.

Open gates with hand and whip.

Hunting.

Continue short and quiet days with hounds.

STAGE C3

RIDING

Repeat Stages C1, C2.

Mount without stirrups on either side.

Free walk on a loose rein.

Trot circles of 10 yards diameter.

Trot 3 loops.

Turn on the haunches at the walk (Pirouette).

Simple change of leg.

Balance and Collection.

Ride Pony Club Dressage Test.

Reins in one hand.

Double Ride.

Jumping a variety of fences and ditches with and without stirrups at all paces.

Jump up and down hill and on slopes.

Jump drops; slip reins if necessary.

Jump 'In and Out' and awkward fences.

Improve seat and position.

Stirrups may be shortened for jumping.

Relaxing exercises. Elementary show jumping and hunter trials.

Independent work.

Crack a whip on pony.

Repetition before Test B.

Games: Changing pony race. Lead pony race. Other competitions. Polocrosse. Cushion polo.

OTHER INSTRUCTION

Hunting. Farming and Hunting. Farm Ride. The Field. Getting to the meet. Time. Dress. Manners and etiquette.

Riding to hounds.

The Master's control of the Field.

Recognise when a horse is lame or sick.

Elementary First Aid.

Know how to carry out the most common types of treatment prescribed by Veterinary Surgeons for wounds, ailments and lameness.

See "The Manual of Horsemanship".

Some knowledge of stabling, ventilation, light, drainage, shelter and warmth.

Revision.

Revision of Highway Code.

TRAINING OF PONY

Repeat Stages D1 to C2.

Free walk on loose rein.

Circles (10 yards diameter) at trot.

Loops at trot.

Turn on the haunches at the walk (Pirouette).

Simple change of leg.

Jump up and down hill; drops; 'In and Out'.

Commence elementary show jumping.

Independent work. Gallop. Crack whip.

Hunting. Longer days and bigger fences.

Gallop smoothly and quietly.

Take Test for Standard 'B' at age of 14 or over. Members under 14 are not eligible for this Test.

STAGE B1

After passing Standard 'B' the objective is to become an active and effective horseman, able to apply the aids efficiently, capable of riding an unknown horse and able to teach a horse the aids.

RIDING

Repeat Stage C3.

Turn on haunches

Half pass.

Canter circle 10 yards diameter.

Rein back.

Train for Dressage Tests.

Jump every sort of fence, blind and other ditches, with and without reins and stirrups, at all paces.

Relaxing exercises Ride 'hot', 'sticky', 'nappy' and 'refusing' horses.

Sit awkward jumps—fences at difficult distances.

Style, polish and ease when jumping.

Meeting fences right'.

Show jumping competitions and Hunter Trials. Showing a horse in the ring.

Independent and individual work.

Accurate judgement of pace (timing between milestones and telegraph poles).

Games: Relay race, with or without jumps, singly or in pairs.

Polo.

OTHER INSTRUCTION

Feeding. Watering.

Forage and Bedding.

Care and Feeding of a sick horse.

See "Horsemanship for the Pony Club".

Practical grooming, clipping, plaiting and trimming.

Stables and stable construction.

Care of saddlery.

Further instruction in bitting.

Hunting: The Hunter, type and breeding, feeding, condition, exercise, training and riding.

TRAINING OF PONY

The next stage is to improve the standard of training of the pony.

The pony should be keen and responsive, but submissive and obedient. There should be soft and light contact with the bit and no throwing up of the head.

Develop freedom of movement and action, smoothness and, above all, straightness.

Jump all kinds of fences at all paces. Go kindly alone and in company.

Repeat stages D1 to C3.

Half-pass.

Circle (10 yards diameter) at canter.

Loop at the canter. Rein back.

Jump larger and more varied fences at fast as well as slow paces.

Bigger show jumping fences (up to 3ft. 6 ins.) and hunter trials. A higher standard of performance.

Hunting: The pony should go out regularly and be improving and gaining experience.

STAGE B2

RIDING	OTHER INSTRUCTION	TRAINING OF PONY
Repeat Stage B1.	Health, condition and exercise.	Repeat Stages D1 to B1.
Strike off to canter on straight line.	Shoeing.	Improve and perfect Stage B1.
Canter one loop without change of leg.	Minor ailments (more advanced than in Stage C3).	The pony should now be able to jump any kind of fence within his capacity. If he shows any aptitude for show-jumping he should jump a 4 ft. course and take part in competitions.
Ride B.H.S. Preliminary Dressage Test.	Care of a corn-fed horse and pony.	
Jumping.	Care of a corn-fed horse and pony before and after hunting, horse trials and long distance rides.	Hunting : As in B1.
Continue Stage B1.		Concentrate on weak points in training.
Improve and strengthen seat, position and style.	Revision.	
Further practice in Show Jumping and Hunter Trials over more difficult and wider fences.	Hunting: Learn duties of Hunt servants (e.g. understudy at Children's meet).	
A higher standard of independent work at faster paces, alone and in company.	Go out stopping.	
Handiness and manners.	After hunting, care of hounds and horses.	
Repetition before Test A.		
Games: Mock pig sticking or balloon breaking. Bending race with jump. Gymkhana events. Paddock Polo.		
Hunting. Further practice and experience in riding to hounds on different horses.		

Take Test for Standard 'A' at the age of 16 or over.

STAGE A

This stage is for those who have reached Standard 'A'—the highest award of the Pony Club. Apart from improving their riding and widening their experience, they should aim at becoming expert trainers of young horses and instructors in riding.

RIDING

Take part in Jumping Competitions, Hunter Trials, Polo, Horse Shows, Point-to-Points, Horse Trials or some such activity.

In general continue to work at improvement of riding and widen experience.

Ride well to hounds on an unknown horse; choose own place to jump. Give leads to children who are in difficulties. Generally be useful—opening gates, helping those in trouble, catching loose horses, turning back cattle, SHUTTING GATES

OTHER INSTRUCTION

Aim at becoming an Instructor. In the meantime act as Asst. Instructor at Rallies, giving demonstrations and helping with backward individuals or awkward ponies.

In particular study principles of instruction and the various lessons.

Attend Instructors' Courses.

TRAINING OF PONY

The horse should be trained as a hunter, show-jumper, show horse, or for Hunter Trials, Horse Trials, or Point-to-Points.

APPENDIX XI

STANDARDS OF EFFICIENCY

INTRODUCTION

Included in the following pages are Test Sheets for Pony Club Standards 'D', 'C', 'B' and 'A'. The pamphlet, "The Pony Club Standards of Efficiency", is available to Test Examiners, Visiting Commissioners, District Commissioners and Branch and Visiting Instructors.

The individual sheets should be given to members who are potential candidates and who will thus have full information as to the subjects in which they will be examined.

When testing candidates, examiners are asked to confine their questions to the relevant syllabus, taking a selection of subjects from that syllabus, and to base their requirements on the teachings of the following books :

  (i) "The Manual of Horsemanship"

  (ii) "Training the Young Pony"

  (iii) "Keeping a Pony at Grass"

  (iv) The pamphlet "Riding and Road Sense".

Permission to take a Test should be withheld until such time as there is a reasonable chance of the necessary standard having been attained. This is of particular importance in regard to Tests 'B' and 'A'. It permits all four tests to be properly spaced through a member's Pony Club career. It avoids waste of examiners' time and the disappointment of failure by an unnecessary number of candidates.

For each standard an Efficiency Certificate is awarded. These are obtainable free of charge from Pony Club Headquarters (See list of supplies, etc., in Pony Club Year Book).

Awards must be approved and all certificates signed by both the examiner and the District Commissioner of the Branch to which the candidate belongs.

The whole test for any standard must be passed on one occasion.

Examiners should bear in mind that Horsemastership is as important as the riding part of the tests.

Members may not be tested for Certificates in another Branch without the consent of the District Commissioner of the Branch to which they belong.

Tests create enthusiasm and ensure progress. At all mounted instructional Rallies examiners should be available to take tests for 'D' Standard. Tests for 'C' Standard can be arranged at certain preselected Rallies.

Tests for 'B' Standard are normally held once or twice a year, being taken by examiners from outside the Branch. Tests for 'A' Standard are arranged regionally and all details supplied to District Commissioners.

Sudden decisions to put members up for a Test should be avoided. Candidates should be given notice to allow them to prepare for their tests.

Those who persist that they should have precise details are looking upon these tests in the wrong light. The Syllabus of Instruction (in the "Instructors' Handbook") is a guide to those concerned as to what potential candidates should have been taught prior to presenting themselves for testing. A study of the Syllabus will make the spacing of tests quite clear and should prevent the mistake of allowing members to take the tests too young. Apart

from 'A' Standard for which the minimum age is 16 years, and
'B' Standard for which the minimum age is 14 years, there are no
other limits laid down, but in general, adherence to the years suggested in the Syllabus is strongly advised: e.g., 'D' about 8 to 9
years ; 'C' about 11 to 12 years ; 'B' 14 or over ; 'A' 16 or over.

Examiners are absolutely within their rights to refuse to be ex-
ploited as a means for telling hopeless candidates (or candidates'
parents) that they are no good ! If, in the opinion of the examiner,
a candidate is hopeless, the test should be discontinued.

'D' STANDARD TEST

All arrangements for carrying out tests for 'D' Standard,
including the appointment of an examiner, will be made by the
District Commissioner or his representative.

The Test Sheet forms the syllabus for this Test. Simple games
could well be incorporated as part of the Test to make it less of an
ordeal. No special facilities required.

'C' STANDARD TEST

The examiner for a 'C' Test must be an official of a Branch of
the Pony Club, or a Visiting Commissioner or Visiting Instructor.

All arrangements for carrying out tests for 'C' Standard, including the appointment of an examiner, will be made by the District
Commissioner. Plenty of opportunity should be given to candidate
and examiner to prepare for the test by advance notice.

Candidates should be capable of expressing themselves better
than in the previous test, but if the examiner can really find out,
by assisting, how much the candidate knows as opposed to what
he does not know, so much the better.

The examiner should be satisfied that the candidate has a practical and not only a theoretical knowledge of how to look after a pony.

Facilities for 'C' Test

(1) Candidates ride their own ponies (or ponies they have hired or borrowed for the occasion).

(2) An enclosed field with several small jumps (cavalletti are useful).

(3) A manege.

(4) Saddlery, grooming kit, etc.

(5) Some forage.

'B' STANDARD TEST

The examiner for a 'B' Test must be a Visiting Commissioner or Visiting Instructor or someone approved for the purpose by the Pony Club Organisation Committee.

Notes for Examiners

Phase 1.   Have a talk to the candidate and ascertain name, age, school or anything else to 'break the ice'.   Question about the pony and find out how much the candidate knows about it.

Phase 2.   Let the candidate mount and ride the pony in the open at walk, trot, canter and gallop and jump, all done in the candidate's own time.   During this phase make up your mind as to whether the candidate looks 'at home' on a horse and would be no disgrace to be seen in the hunting field on your well-mannered horse.   If the candidate passes this stage then, on the same pony or on one you have selected, pass on to Phase 3, which is a test of knowledge as well as of execution.

Phase 3. (Most easily carried out in a lettered arena). Walk, trot (rising and sitting) and canter at ordinary and extended paces. Increase and decrease of pace, circles at the trot. Turns on the move. Turns on the forehand from the halt. Canter on a named leg. Simple change of leg at the canter by trotting a few paces before the change.

Do not expect perfection, but make sure that the candidate understands the movement required by you, and that he or she not only applies the correct aids, but is able to explain what aid was applied for any particular movement, and why.

Facilities for 'B' Test

(1) Candidates riding own ponies (or ponies they have hired or borrowed for the occasion) will be expected to change ponies during the Test.

(2) An enclosed field with several jumps, natural and artificial, including cavalletti.

(3) A manege marked out as for a Dressage Test.

(4) A properly equipped stable with saddlery, including a double bridle, grooming kit, stable utensils, rugs, bandages, a headcollar, etc., all of which must fit the horse provided.

(5) Different items of forage.

'A' STANDARD TEST

The Examiners for an 'A' Test are appointed from a special panel by Pony Club Headquarters. The examination is arranged at various centres by H.Q., where horses and facilities are available.

The candidate should show the confidence and ability that comes from practical experience in riding and handling different types of horses. The aim of the examiner is to find out what the candidate knows and can do as opposed to exposing his weaknesses. The

candidate should give the examiner confidence that, should
he have to look after the latter's horse for a period of several days,
he would carry out instructions implicitly and safely, knowing
when to call the vet., riding and caring for the horse according to
the recognised principles taught in the Pony Club, and handing it
back with its training and physical condition unimpaired, or even
improved.

Although no doubt examiners will have their own form of
marking these tests, it is suggested that District Commissioners
and candidates find it of great benefit if they are handed the results
in such a way that they are able to see their strength or weakness in
various subjects. As a guide, an assessment might be given under
the following headings :

C— Poor	B— Below average	A— Good
C+ Not up to standard	B+ Average	A+ Very good

This would imply that a candidate obtaining a C in any subject
must fail.

It is strongly recommended that either the District Commissioner, the Chief Instructor or another knowledgeable member of
the Local Committee is deputed to accompany the candidate to
the test. Opportunities will be given for the Branch Representative to discuss the result and the reasons for success or failure,
with the examiners.

Nominations must be made to Headquarters on the cards
provided giving first and, if possible, alternative choice of dates.
A fee is payable by the Branch for each candidate nominated.
The nominations must be signed by the District Commissioner
who is required to state (as in the Pony Club Year Book) :

(a) Name, address, telephone number and date of birth of the
candidate.

(b) That the candidate has been tested riding various horses and ponies and is up to the standard required according to Pony Club teaching.

(c) That the candidate has been trained in the other subjects required for this Test, and is up to the standard required.

(d) That in case of doubt the candidate has been reported as up to standard by somebody with experience of this Test.

Branches will be informed when their candidates have been accepted for examination and will be sent details of the time and place of the examination. Early notification must be given if any candidate is unable to attend.

If the number of candidates waiting exceeds the number of vacancies, the older candidates will normally be given priority.

No candidate can normally be included in any examination that takes place less than six weeks after receipt of the nomination. Therefore, early nomination is advisable. A candidate nominated not less than three months before his or her 21st birthday, may take the *next* test held in the area, even if this takes place after the candidate has become 21 years of age.

Facilities for 'A' Test

An examination centre is chosen where the following is available:

(1) Several horses of varying stages of training, different temperaments (e.g. keen, free, sluggish, 'nappy') and ability, are required for candidates to ride. It is important that a trained horse is available. They will not bring their own horses.

(2) An indoor school as well as outdoor paddocks and jumps.

(3) A properly equipped stable with saddlery, including a double bridle, rugs, bandages, headcollar, all of which must fit the horse provided ; also grooming kit, stable utensils, types of forage, etc.

TEST SHEET
'D' STANDARD

OBJECTIVE

To achieve confidence in handling and riding a pony.
To be keen to improve and learn.

RIDING

Mount and Dismount.
Correct position in the saddle.
How to hold the reins.
Ride without a leading rein.

ROAD SENSE

How to ride along and cross a road; say "thank you".

HORSEMASTERSHIP

Approach and handle a pony correctly.
Catch pony and put on headcollar.
Proper way to give a pony an apple or carrot.
Lead a pony in hand.
Name simple points of the pony.
Name different parts of saddle and bridle.

READ

"The Manual of Horsemanship"

Points of the Horse...	page XVI
Mounting and Dismounting	pages 1 - 2
The Rider's position	pages 2 - 6
How to hold the reins	pages 10 - 11
Saddle and Bridle	pages 89 - 92, 104 - 105
Handling ponies	pages 126 - 129

"Riding and Road Sense" (*pamphlet*)

Take Test for Standard 'D' at age of 8 or 9.

TEST SHEET
'C' STANDARD

OBJECTIVE

To attain a firm seat independent of the reins and to apply simple aids correctly.

To have a knowledge of the care and working of a pony off grass.

To be in control of the pony on the roads and in the countryside. To have a proper regard for road sense, safety and courtesy and for country lore.

RIDING

Turnout of pony and rider.

Mount and Dismount.

Correct position in the saddle.

Hold the reins correctly.

Alter stirrups when mounted.

Tighten and loosen girth when mounted.

Physical exercises at halt and walk.

Position at walk, trot, canter and gallop.

Use of seat, legs and hands as aids to increase and decrease pace.

Simple turns and circles at walk and trot.

Aids for the canter on a named leg on a circle.

Walk with a long rein.

Ride up and down hill.

Independent work in the open.

Walk and trot over heavy poles as a preliminary to jumping.

Ride over cavalletti and very small fences and ditches.

ROAD SENSE AND COUNTRY LORE

Riding on the roads.

Knowledge of the Highway Code and correct signals.

Riding in the countryside, and across farmland.

HORSEMASTERSHIP

Points of the horse, colours and markings.

Care and working of a horse off grass.

Elementary feeding, watering and cleanliness of the horse.

Lead horse in hand at walk and trot and turn about.

Know how to take a horse in and out of a horse-box.

Picking up and picking out the feet.

Names and uses of the essential grooming kit.

Know how to saddle and bridle.

Elementary care and cleaning of saddlery.

Know when a horse needs shoeing and what to look for in a newly-shod foot.

Have some elementary knowledge of the treatment of minor wounds.

Recognise when a horse is lame.

Know the main indications of health in the horse.

READ the following Pony Club Publications:

"Keeping a Pony at Grass". The whole book.

"The Manual of Horsemanship"

The points of the Horse	...	...	...	page XVI
The Rider's position ...	...	...	...	pages I - II
The Aids	...	...	...	... pages 13 - 22

"Riding and Road Sense" (*pamphlet*)

Take Test for Standard 'C' at age of 11 or 12.

TEST SHEET

'B' STANDARD

OBJECTIVE

To become an active horseman who knows the reasons for what he is doing.

To ride over fences at all paces.

To gain practical experience and knowledge of the care of a stabled pony and of a pony at grass.

To be capable of riding a well-mannered horse or pony out hunting, in horse trials, or on a long distance ride, to look after a pony before, during and after the day's hunting or other activity.

To ride intelligently and with due regard for others on the roads and in the country, with a knowledge of pace, distance and discipline when riding alone and in groups.

RIDING

Turn-out of pony and rider.

Mount and dismount on either side.

Position, at walk, trot, canter and gallop.

Sitting trot, rising trot on either diagonal, change of diagonal.

Physical exercises at halt, walk and trot.

Application of the aids for increase and decrease of pace, turns and circles, rein back.

Turns on the forehand from the halt ;   turns on the haunches at the walk (Pirouette).

Stand still.   Salute.

Free walk on long rein and with a loose rein.

Change of leg at the canter, through a trot.

Ride with reins in one hand.

Open gate with hand and whip.

Ride up and down steep hills and banks.

Independent work.

Bits and their uses. Ride with double bridle.

Elementary Riding School drill.

How to show a pony in the ring.

Understand the meaning of balance and collection.

Jump a variety of fences and ditches, at trot and canter.

Jump up and down hill ; jump drop fences, slipping reins as necessary ; jump doubles and awkward fences.

ROAD SENSE AND COUNTRY LORE

Knowledge of the Highway Code.

Proper behaviour on the roads under all circumstances.

HORSEMASTERSHIP

Good and bad points of conformation.

Practical care and working of a pony off grass.

Knowledge of the care and working of a corn-fed, stabled horse and of exercising and getting a horse fit.

Know principles of watering and feeding and be able to put them into practice. Have a knowledge of the different items of forage.

Know the articles of grooming kit and be able to use them.

Be able to rug up and bandage correctly.

Have some knowledge of stabling — ventilation, light, drainage, shelter and warmth.

Shoeing. Know Something of the structure of the horse's foot.

Know the names of the farrier's tools and their uses.

Be able to name the parts of the foot, the parts of the horse's shoes and the different types of shoe.

Be able to fit saddlery.

Know how to care for and clean saddlery.

Be capable of loading and unloading a horse in a box or trailer
and preparing a horse for travel.

Know when a horse is lame, sick or in poor condition and know
the most common causes of these ailments.

Elementary first aid.

Be able to carry out prescribed treatment of wounds, ailments
and lameness.

READ

Pony Club Publications as under:

"The Manual of Horsemanship"

"Training the Young Pony"

"Keeping a Pony at Grass"

"Riding and Road Sense"

Take Test for 'B' Standard at age of 14 or over. Members under
14 are not eligible for this Test.

TEST SHEET
'A' STANDARD

This is the highest award of the Pony Club.

The Certificate is awarded in two Grades, "Pass" and "Honours"

OBJECTIVE

The 'A' Test is the highest award of the Pony Club and provides a comprehensive examination in Horsemanship and Horsemastership for well-trained and experienced senior Members and Associates.

Candidates must be able to show that they can carry out in practice all they have learnt from the Pony Club publications and their instructors, in a logical sequence.

They should be capable of taking charge of corn-fed stabled horses or ponies, for a limited period, and, with some supervision, of carrying out their systematic training.

Candidates must have had experience with horses as well as ponies.

STANDARD REQUIRED

RIDING

A correct position, a firm, independent seat and a high standard of riding are necessary to obtain the 'A' Certificate.

Candidates must:

Be relaxed and ride with confidence, style and polish both on the flat and over fences and have a well-developed sense of rhythm and pace.

Be active and effective horsemen, able to apply the "aids" efficiently and to ride all the movements described in the "Manual of Horsemanship" and "Training the Young Horse and Pony".

Understand what is meant by the expressions "free forward movement", "accept the Bit", "balance", etc., and appreciate their importance.

Be able to ride unknown horses over any type of fence at all appropriate paces and also to ride green or awkward and refusing horses with understanding.

Be able to ride horses correctly at the gallop.

Be able, with some supervision, to carry out the basic training of a young horse or pony in accordance with the principles laid down in "Training the Young Horse and Pony", to correct faults in an older horse, improve his way of going and explain what they are doing and why.

HORSEMASTERSHIP

The 'A' Certificate implies the ability to take sole charge of corn-fed, stabled horses or ponies for at least a fortnight; this in turn means that a Candidate has in fact looked after a horse or pony, has the practical experience, is efficient and does not merely possess theoretical knowledge.

The syllabus for this Standard is contained in the "Manual of Horsemanship" and may be summarised as: handling horses and ponies; the grass-kept pony; stable construction; clothing; grooming; care and fitting of saddlery; clipping and trimming; feeding and watering; forage and bedding; the foot and shoeing; health, condition, fitness and exercise; recognition of lameness and minor ailments, and their veterinary treatment; the identification of horses and ponies, breed, colour and markings. Candidates will be expected to demonstrate practical knowledge and efficiency in all aspects of horse-care in and out of the stables.

FORM OF THE TEST

There are four phases to the Test.

OUTSIDE RIDING

During this phase, candidates have the opportunity of riding
three or four different horses.

Having been allocated their first horse, they are allowed
5 - 10 minutes to try it out, on the flat and over a few small
fences. While doing this, they are expected to assess the
horse — its good and weak points, to be thinking for what
work it is most suited, and how it could be schooled to give
a better performance and ride.

Candidates are then asked to "show" the horse to the examiners
at all paces, jump a few selected obstacles and talk to the
examiner about the horse and the way it goes. This discussion usually lasts for about 5 minutes, and the examiners
hope to hear practical, common-sense answers, which
would give them confidence that the candidate has the
knowledge and capability of improving that particular horse
or any other that he/she might be given to ride.

Candidates then change onto at least two more horses, and
depending on the facilities available, jump a short cross-
country or show jumping course on each horse.

INSIDE RIDING

Candidates who satisfy the examiners in the Outside Riding,
come forward in the afternoon to ride two or three schooled
horses, indoors.

They will again be given the opportunity of trying out these
horses before being asked to perform some of the simple
school movements, such as medium walk, working and
medium trot and canter; halts; transitions; some lengthen-

ing and shortening of the stride; simple changes of leg; turns on the forehand; half-pirouettes at the walk, leg-yielding, etc.

The examiners will probably ask the Candidates to comment on the way the horses are going and the manner in which they perform the movements. Failure to perform the required movements does not necessarily mean failure of the Test.

The points the examiners look for are: how the Candidates apply the aids; that they can maintain an even balanced pace, with the horse showing the correct "outline", and feel when it is actively carrying and using itself to the best of its ability. They should be able to deal successfully with negative responses, or resistances, and offer positive suggestions as to how these simple movements could be achieved.

HORSEMASTERSHIP

This part of the Test takes place either before or after the Outside Riding within the general area of the stableyard, including a tack room, with varieties of saddlery, shoes, farriers tools, etc., and a medicine chest; a forage barn with samples of forage and a horse in a loose box with rugs, bandages, grooming kit, stable gear and saddlery.

Candidates are given practical tasks to carry out as well as questions and answers, often in the form of discussion.

TRAINING THE YOUNG HORSE

The final phase of the Test is a discussion with the examiner on Training the Young Horse. Candidates are expected to know the principles of handling, lungeing, backing and preliminary training of a young horse, using the equipment and methods recommended by the Pony Club.

They are not asked to demonstrate during this phase, but obviously are able to talk much more convincingly if they have had practical experience.

READ

Pony Club Publications as under:

"Manual of Horsemanship"

"Keeping a Pony at Grass"

"Training the Young Horse and Pony"

All pamphlets published by the B.H.S. for the PONY CLUB.

Suggested further reading:

"Dressage Rules and Official Procedure for Dressage Competitions" (B.H.S.)

"First Aid Hints for the Horse Owner" (W. E. Lyon)

"Grassland Management for Horse and Pony Owners" (B.H.S.)

"Veterinary Notes for the Horse Owner" (Paperback — Hayes)

"Know your Horse" (Codrington)

"Animal Management" (H.M.S.O., 1955)

"Anatomy of the Horse" (Dr. Smith)

Take Test for Standard 'A' at age of 16 or over.

INDEX

OTHER OFFICIAL PUBLICATIONS

British Horse Society Publications
"RULES FOR DRESSAGE"
"RULES FOR COMBINED TRAINING"
*"RIDING" by Mrs. V. D. S. Williams

Pony Club Publications
*"THE MANUAL OF HORSEMANSHIP"
*"TRAINING THE YOUNG HORSE AND PONY"
*"KEEPING A PONY AT GRASS" by Mrs. O. Faudel-Phillips, F.I.H.
*"MOUNTED GAMES AND GYMKHANAS"
*"QUIZ QUESTIONS"
*"POLO FOR THE PONY CLUB"
*"A GUIDE TO THE PURCHASE OF CHILDREN'S PONIES"
*"RIDING TO HOUNDS"
"NOTES FOR FIVE-MINUTE LECTURES—FOXHUNTING"
"THE PONY CLUB YEAR BOOK"

*"BASIC TRAINING FOR YOUNG HORSES & PONIES" by
Mrs. V. D. S. Williams
*"THE FOOT AND SHOEING" by Major C. Davenport, F.R.C.V.S.
"THE GENERAL PURPOSE SEAT" by Col. The Hon. C. G. Cubitt,
D.S.O., T.D., D.L. and Col. G. T. Hurrell, O.B.E.
*"BITS AND BITTING" by Col. The Hon. C. G. Cubitt
*"THE AIDS AND THEIR APPLICATION" by Col. The Hon. C. G. Cubitt,
D.S.O., T.D., D.L.
Film Strips are also available for each of these titles

An up-to-date price list of Pony Club publications is shown in the
Pony Club Year Book, issued annually, and is available from Headquarters, address as below.

These and other publications connected with the horse are
available from

THE BRITISH HORSE SOCIETY
National Equestrian Centre, Kenilworth
Warwickshire, CV8 2LR

These are available from
BARRON'S
113 Crossways Park Drive
Woodbury, New York 11797